CRIME TIME

CRIME TIME

Twenty True Tales of Murder,
Madness, and Mayhem

J. NORTH CONWAY

Guilford, Connecticut

An imprint of The Rowman & Littlefield Publishing Group, Inc.
4501 Forbes Blvd., Ste. 200
Lanham, MD 20706
www.rowman.com

Distributed by NATIONAL BOOK NETWORK

British Library Cataloguing in Publication Information available

Library of Congress Cataloging-in-Publication Data
Names: Conway, J. North (Jack North), author.
Title: Crime time : twenty true tales of murder, madness, and mayhem / Jack Conway.
Description: Guilford, Connecticut : Lyons Press, [2021] | Includes bibliographical references and index. | Summary: "CRIME TIME is a collection of 20 riveting, page-turning historic true crime stories from 1724 to 1913 covering a host of monstrous American and English criminals, their crimes, and their punishment"—Provided by publisher.
Identifiers: LCCN 2020055134 (print) | LCCN 2020055135 (ebook) | ISBN 9781493052882 (hardcover ; alk. paper) | ISBN 9781493052899 (epub)
Subjects: LCSH: Criminals—Case studies. | Crime—Case studies. | Murder—Case studies.
Classification: LCC HV6245 .C65 2021 (print) | LCC HV6245 (ebook) | DDC 364.152/3092241—dc23
LC record available at https://lccn.loc.gov/2020055134
LC ebook record available at https://lccn.loc.gov/2020055135

ISBN 978-1-4930-5288-2 (cloth: alk. paper)
ISBN 978-1-4930-5289-9 (electronic)

♾️™ The paper used in this publication meets the minimum requirements of American National Standard for Information Sciences—Permanence of Paper for Printed Library Materials, ANSI/NISO Z39.48–1992.

"Though it abide a year, or two, or three,
Murder will out, this is my conclusion . . ."

—Geoffrey Chaucer, "The Prioress's Tale"

The Canterbury Tales, 1387

Several of these stories originally appeared as

"Meet 'The Queen of Thieves' Marm Mandelbaum, New York City's First Mob Boss," The Daily Beast, *2014.*

"The High Society Bank Robber of the 1800s," The Daily Beast, *2014.*

"The Bicycle Bandit," The Providence Journal, *2000.*

Contents

Murder Will Out

An Introduction

This book is a compendium of riveting, page-turning historically true crime stories covering twenty monstrous American and English criminals, their crimes, and their punishments. The stories involve murder, mayhem, robbery, poisoning, kidnapping, and just about everything in between, committed in the name of madness, money, love, greed, and self-preservation.

It does not include stories of people as famous as London's Jack the Ripper or Fall River, Massachusetts's Lizzie Borden. To use a bad pun, their stories have been done to death. It includes other less-well-known criminals—men, women, and children, whose gruesome tales have been obscured by the passage of time but whose crimes are no less heinous.

Crime is generally defined as an offense against public law. In 1911, English legal scholar William Blake Odgers defined crime as follows: "A wrongful act of such a kind that the State deems it necessary, in the interests of the public, to repress it; for its repetition would be harmful to the community as a whole." If we are to adhere to Odgers's definition of crime, insomuch as we need to repress it in the desired hope of eradicating its repetition, then we must as well illuminate these lesser-known crimes to be better able to deal with their horrifying recurrence. If we remain ignorant of particular crimes and their historical significance, how can we ever hope to adequately address and deal with them as a society?

In each of these stories, the crime and criminals were found out through one means or another—"murder will out." That phrase was first reportedly stated in Geoffrey Chaucer's *The Canterbury Tales*. It maintained the belief that murder was such a horrible thing that God would not allow it to be concealed for very long and that a person who commits a murder would be found out, often through their own unintended behavior.

Within these pages you will discover the story of the first bank robbery in America, as well as the largest one. You will find a young man who was hanged not because of any crimes he committed but because he embarrassed the authorities and they needed to make an example of him. You will discover young children and the mentally disabled who were hanged for their crimes, including petty theft, even the theft of a small basket of strawberries. You will discover physicians and nurses who, despite their oath to save lives, killed family, friends, and patients by poisoning them. You will discover ministers who resorted to murder to cover up the sexual abuses of the members of their congregations. You will discover a clan of thieves who terrorized communities for over sixty years. You will discover a Harvard University medical school professor who murdered to conceal his debts and a New York City man charged for a gruesome murder mimicking Jack the Ripper. You will read about a Jewish immigrant who rose to the top of the crime world and an Irish immigrant who tried to rise to be the matriarch of a family by savagely murdering the current wife. You will find well-to-do members of society who resorted to murder to escape their past and to improve their futures as well as a young man from a prominent family who robbed stores at gunpoint and eluded authorities by speeding away on a bicycle. You will read about America's first recorded kidnapping for ransom as well as the ransom for the remains of a dead man. And you will discover a beautiful young woman criminal who decided to turn her life around but found that her past had caught up with her.

Crime stories must go hand in hand with punishment and in each of these stories, punishment was meted out, although, in some instances, not quite as fitting as one might have hoped for. In some cases, given the circumstances, the punishment led to dramatic changes in the process of the legal system, including opening up the debate in America over the death penalty, and legislating juvenile prosecution and kidnapping as a federal offense.

CHAPTER I

Gentleman Jack

Jack Shepard, 1724

There was hardly a prison in 1724 London that could hold escape artist extraordinaire Jack Sheppard.

There wasn't a prison in London that eighteenth-century thief and highwayman Gentleman Jack Sheppard couldn't escape from, except one—when he became the prisoner of love.

Jack Sheppard broke out of the second-floor cell at St. Giles jail in London by breaking through the wooden ceiling and lowering himself to the ground with a rope made from bedclothes. Sheppard was small and slight but amazingly strong. Although he was still wearing iron handcuffs and chains, he hid them and casually joined the posse that was busily pursuing the newly escaped prisoner—himself. He was able to distract the posse by pointing to the rooftop and proclaiming he could see the escaped prisoner. Not knowing they had been duped, the posse followed in pursuit and Sheppard escaped into the night.

Sheppard had an uncanny knack for prison escapes and defiance of London's pompous authorities, which made him a hero among the commoners of London in 1724. He captured the imagination of Londoners and was the darling of newspapers, then termed "broadsheets," for his remarkable escapes from a number of London prisons.

Sheppard began his criminal career working for Jonathan Wild. Wild, known as "The Thief Taker General," operated on both sides of the law. On one hand, he was a public-spirited crimefighter, chasing down and apprehending criminals, and on the other, he operated a criminal empire across London. In order to keep tabs on his vast criminal empire, Wild kept a ledger of thieves, burglars, and highwaymen in his employ. Those on his roster who were active had a cross next to their name. Those who became his enemy, as Sheppard did, he put a second cross next to their name, indicating he was going to turn them in to the authorities. Thus, the term "double cross," indicating betrayal, originated with Wild.

Because of Sheppard's cunning as a thief, Wild courted him, wanting Sheppard to become part of his criminal empire. However, he demanded that Sheppard exclusively give him all of his stolen plunder to sell. Since Sheppard could often make more money selling his stolen goods to other buyers and sellers of stolen property, he refused Wild's entreaties, angering Wild, and making him an avowed enemy of the London crime boss.

Jack Sheppard was only twenty-two years old when he was first arrested in April 1724 and was held on the top floor of St. Giles jail in London. He was arrested when his older brother, Tom, betrayed him to authorities. Sheppard and Tom had broken into a workshop and stolen tools. Although Jack managed to get away, Tom was caught. Tom had been arrested twice before and was facing the death penalty since execution was the punishment in England at the time for third-time offenders. In order to escape his punishment, Tom informed on his brother. It did not take Sheppard long to escape and elude his captors.

After his escape, he returned to Piccadilly to join his mistress, Bess Lyon. When he arrived home, he discovered she had been arrested and was being held back at St. Giles, the jail Sheppard had just recently escaped from. Lyon was a young prostitute that Sheppard met at The Black Lion Tavern in London. The tavern was a hangout for known criminals, including, Joseph "Blueskin" Blake. Blake's nickname was given to him because of the port wine birthmark that adorned his face. Blake and Sheppard became friends and partners in crime. When Blake informed Sheppard that Lyon was being held at St. Giles, they returned to the prison to free her. When the officer at the jail refused to let Sheppard in to see her, he had Blake caused a distraction and broke Lyon out of her cell. All three were able to escape.

Before he fell in with the likes of Jonathan Wild, "Blueskin" Blake, and Bess Lyon, Sheppard was a carpenter, but his affinity to alcohol and his affection for Lyon got the best of him. With Lyon's encouragement, and Blake's help, Sheppard embraced a life of crime and he found himself good at it. His first theft was in 1723, when he stole two silver spoons from an employer. Since this minor crime went undetected and unpunished, he moved on to larger crimes, including burglary and highway robbery.

In May 1724, Sheppard was arrested a second time for pickpocketing and was held overnight at Saint Ann's prison in Soho. Bess Lyon went to visit him there the next day, but Jonathan Wild alerted the authorities, informing them that Lyon was Sheppard's mistress. She was arrested as well and locked up in the same cell. They were then sent to the notorious Newgate Prison in Central London to await trial. Within a week, they escaped by filing through their manacles and knocking out a bar from the

cell window. Once again, Sheppard used knotted bedshee
climb down the prison walls to the ground, carrying Lyon ...
Although surrounded by a twenty-foot wall, Sheppard and Lyon climbed
the prison wall and escaped. News of his amazing escape spread quickly
and accounts of his escape with Lyon on his back appeared in many London newspapers. The feat made Sheppard a newfound hero for London's
poor and working class.

After escaping from Newgate, Sheppard and Blake went on a burglary spree, including burgling Sheppard's former employer, William
Kneebone. Learning of Sheppard's escape and subsequent burglaries,
Jonathan Wild became obsessed with capturing him since Sheppard still
refused to become part of his criminal empire and fence his stolen merchandise exclusively with him. Unfortunately for Sheppard, the man he
did sell his stolen loot to, William Field, was one of Wild's men who
informed on them.

Sheppard and Blake also tried their hands as highwaymen—robbers
who hold up travelers and steal their money and property. During one of
these robberies, Sheppard earned the sobriquet "Gentleman Jack" when
he declined to take a gold locket from a man he held at gunpoint along
a deserted road. The victim claimed the locket contained the only picture
of his mother.

After a series of daring robberies, Sheppard and Blake went into
hiding at a small brandy shop that was owned and operated by Blake's
mother. Wild decided that Bess Lyon would know Sheppard's whereabouts. He plied her with countless drinks. Not knowing Wild's intentions, she drunkenly betrayed Sheppard and Blake, informing Wild of
their whereabouts. The place was surrounded and the two men were
arrested. Sheppard was again taken to Newgate Prison where he was held
for trial.

Sheppard was prosecuted on three charges of theft at the Central
Criminal Court of England and Wales, commonly known as Old Bailey, but was acquitted on the first two charges due to lack of evidence.
William Kneebone, Jonathan Wild, and William Field all gave evidence
against him on the third charge, the burglary of Kneebone's house. He
was convicted on this charge and sentenced to death. On the very day the

death warrant for Sheppard arrived at the prison, he managed to escape once again.

Bess Lyon and Sheppard's brother, Tom, both of whom had betrayed him in the past, came to the prison to make amends. While Lyon and Tom distracted the prison guards, Sheppard loosened an iron bar in a window and climbed through the gap he had made. Dressed in women's clothing that Lyon had brought with her, Sheppard was smuggled out of Newgate in disguise. He took a boat up the Thames to Westminster where he hid out in an abandoned warehouse. The newspapers once again heralded the amazing escape of "Gentleman Jack" Sheppard.

The more the papers wrote about Sheppard, the more he became a working-class hero. None of Sheppard's crimes involved violence. He only robbed from the rich and he was seemingly able to escape from the authorities at will. All of it enraged Wild. He sent several gangs out to look for Sheppard, but Sheppard managed to evade capture. Infuriated, Wild decided he had been double-crossed by Bess Lyon and Tom Sheppard and sent his most brutal henchman, James Sykes, nicknamed "Hell and Fury," to deal with them. Sheppard left London for a few days while Wild's men continued unsuccessfully to search for him. When he finally returned to London, he learned the body of Bess Lyon had been discovered floating in the Thames with her throat cut. His brother Tom had been arrested, was thrown in prison, and awaited the gallows. While trying to pay his last respects to Lyon, Sheppard was arrested by Wild's men and returned to Newgate Prison.

As his fame grew with each escape, Sheppard became the toast of London. People came from far and wide to visit him at the prison, including both high born and low. One of them was the author Daniel Defoe, author of *Robinson Crusoe*. Defoe wrote an article called "The History of the Remarkable Life of John Sheppard," which appeared in a London newspaper.

The entire city waited with bated breath to see if he could again avoid his final sentence. Although Sheppard boasted that he would escape from Newgate once more, his plans were thwarted when the guards found files and other tools in his cell. He was subsequently transferred to a more secure cell in the prison, clasped in leg irons, and chained to the floor to prevent any further escape attempts. Still, Sheppard persisted in taunting his jailors by showing them how he could use a small nail to unlock his leg irons at will. He continued to goad his guards, making light of his dire circumstances and promising to once more escape. Outside the prison, crowds gathered, lit candles, and cheered him on.

Blake was arrested by Wild's men and thrown in prison, while Sheppard's brother Tom was locked up awaiting execution. At Blake's trial, held at the Old Bailey, Field and Wild testified against him. Although their testimony was inconsistent, Blake was convicted anyway and sentenced to hang. Incensed, Blake leapt out of the docket and attacked Wild in the courtroom, slashing his throat with a pocketknife and causing the courtroom to break into pandemonium.

Wild was lucky to survive the attack. Word of the attack spread to Newgate Prison causing near riots there and in the streets. Using the disturbance to his advantage, Sheppard escaped for the fourth time. Although he was able to unlock his handcuffs, he was still weighed down by his leg irons. He climbed up a chimney and broke through a bar in a grate on top to the roof. He then managed to break through six barred doors leading into the prison chapel. On the chapel roof, he tied blankets together and shimmied down the prison wall, landing in the yard of an adjacent house. The noise disturbed an old woman living there who rushed outside with a musket. She fired at the escaping Sheppard nearly hitting him. The blast from the musket sent the old woman sprawling to the ground. Despite the guards being in close pursuit, Sheppard went back to make sure the old woman was all right. He escaped through the streets, finally hiding out in a cowshed on the outskirts of London.

A sympathetic blacksmith freed Sheppard from his leg irons, but his final period of freedom lasted just two weeks. He disguised himself as a beggar and returned to the city where he broke into a shop and stole a black silk suit, a sword, a powdered wig, and jewelry. Disguised as a gentleman, he found his way to the courtyard of Newgate Prison where in disguise he sadly witnessed the hanging of his brother Tom.

He spent the night drinking in the company of two whores, one of whom betrayed him to the authorities. Sheppard was still drunk when the authorities arrested him on the morning of October 29, 1724. He was locked in a cell where he was watched over by guards at all times. He was also weighted down with approximately 300 pounds of chains and leg irons. He was so celebrated that several prominent people sent a petition to King George I pleading for his death sentence to be commuted. He appeared before the judge on November 10 and was offered the chance to have his sentence reduced if he agreed to inform on his criminal associates. He refused. The next day, Blake, who had been held since his arrest and courtroom attack on Jonathan Wild, was hanged.

On November 16, Sheppard was taken to gallows to be hanged. He planned one more escape on the way there by using a concealed knife to cut through the ropes that bound him, but the knife was discovered by a guard and confiscated. Sheppard was led to the gallows in a procession through the streets of London. He was bound and hauled on the back of a horse-drawn cart. Crowds, estimated at approximately 200,000 people, turned out to view the spectacle. Most came to celebrate Sheppard, hoping for him to pull off one last escape, but that never happened.

The procession stopped at a tavern along the route to the gallows where Sheppard was given a tankard of sherry. He toasted the crowd. When approached by a member of the clergy who asked if he wished to redeem himself, Sheppard reportedly proclaimed, "One file's worth all the Bibles in the World!" There was a carnival-like atmosphere at the gallows. As drums beat and horns blared, a hood was put over Sheppard's head, the noose placed around his neck, and the trap door beneath him released. After hanging for the prescribed fifteen minutes, he was declared dead and his body was cut down. The crowd surged forward to get a closer look at the dead thief and escape artist extraordinaire. Sheppard was buried in the churchyard of St. Martin-in-the-Fields in Trafalgar Square.

Following his death, there was a spectacular public reaction to Sheppard's deeds. Tales of his many escapades appeared throughout London and beyond in a variety of newspapers, pamphlets, broadsheets, and ballads, all devoted to his amazing exploits. His story was adapted for the stage almost immediately. The most prominent play depicting his life was *The Beggar's Opera*, written in 1728 by poet and dramatist John Gay. Two centuries later, *The Beggar's Opera* became the basis of the 1928 *The Threepenny Opera* by Bertolt Brecht and Kurt Weill.

Sheppard's story generated a cultural mania in the mid-1800s. A public alarm arose at the possibility that young people would emulate him. This led to a ban on any plays celebrating Sheppard's exploits. Jonathan Wild's fate was sealed in 1725, when he was arrested and charged with stealing. Several of his own men testified against him. He was subsequently sentenced to death. Although he begged for a reprieve, it was denied. He attempted suicide but failed. Wild was taken to the gallows in late May 1725.

When he was visited in the Castle by the Reverend Mr. Wagstaff, he put on the Face only of a Preparation for his End, as appear'd by his frequent Attempts made upon his Escape, and when he has been press'd to Discover those who put him upon Means of Escaping, and furnish'd him with Implements, he would passionately, and with a Motion of striking, say, ask me no such Questions, one File's worth all the Bibles in the World.

—Daniel Defoe, *The History of the Remarkable Life of John Sheppard: Containing a Particular Account of His Many Robberies and Escapes*, 1724.

CHAPTER 2

Hang'em High

Isaac Frasier, 1768

In 1768, Isaac Frasier, a dim-witted inept thief, was executed for his petty crimes.

Isaac Frasier's criminal escapades earned him the dubious title "The Notorious Frasier," but more than anything, it was his notoriety, not the litany of his petty crimes and burglaries, that led to his execution in Fairfield, Connecticut, in 1768.

Isaac Frasier, a twenty-eight-year-old career criminal and thief, rode to Newtown, Connecticut, where he broke into a tailor's shop twice in the same night. The authorities managed to apprehend him and hold him for trial. He was found guilty and sentenced to a public whipping, his ear cropped, and a capital B branded on his forehead. All of these horrifying punishments were routine and familiar to Yankees of the eighteenth century. The Connecticut Superior Court judge warned him that his next offense would be his last. One more arrest and he would be hanged. It didn't seem to deter Frasier. He headed straight for Massachusetts, where he went on another unsuccessful crime spree, committing a series of robberies and burglaries from one end of the state to the other, and was captured once more, setting the stage for his execution.

Frasier was born on February 9, 1740, in North Kingston, Rhode Island. His father died when he was five years old. His criminal career began when he was six years old when he was caught stealing ears of corn from a neighbor's farm. When he was eight years old, he became an apprentice to a Kingston shoemaker, where he earned little or nothing and was mistreated by the shoemaker who frequently beat him. In order to sustain himself, he took to stealing food from neighbors and shops. When the shoemaker's wife found out what he was doing, she did not make him return the stolen food. Instead, she encouraged the young boy to continue his thefts and to further expand his reach to more than just food. For the next eight years, Frasier, under the guidance of the mistress of the house, honed his skills as a thief and sometime burglar. He shared his ill-gotten gains with the shoemaker's wife in exchange for sharing her bed when the shoemaker was gone. When the shoemaker's business failed, Frasier moved on and at sixteen years of age he joined the army where he reluctantly served in several battles during the French and Indian Wars (1754–1763).

In 1760, he left the army and settled in Newport, Rhode Island, where he engaged in his first major theft—stealing a $500 gold watch. He was immediately arrested on suspicion and on questioning by authorities confessed to the crime and returned the watch to its rightful owner. His punishment came in the form of a public whipping. He then moved to Canaan, where he bought a plot of land and tried his hand at farming. There he met a young woman from a well-known family and they were married, but within two years, the drudgery of home life and the lack of money led him to travel to nearby Woodbury, where he broke into a goldsmith's shop and stole nearly $100 worth of merchandize. He was once again immediately caught, and once again the matter was settled privately. When word of his deed spread to Canaan, he was immediately ostracized by the town. Mortified by the incident, his wife left him.

With no family or friends, Frasier left behind any thought of living a law-abiding life and set out on a crime spree that took him through four states—Connecticut, New York, Massachusetts, and Rhode Island. He burglarized homes and businesses throughout colonial New England and New York, sometimes engaging in the theft of property and goods from the same people several times. Each of his attempts at burglary was thwarted and he was arrested and thrown into jail three times. Each time, Frasier managed to escape. He boasted to his criminal cohorts that there wasn't a jail built that could hold him—at least not for long. Throughout his brief life of petty crime, Frasier was seldom punished because he managed to escape from whatever jail was holding him. He became known as colonial America's most inept burglar but extraordinary escape artist. Frasier's criminal escapades earned him the dubious title of "The Notorious Frasier."

After being apprehended for breaking into the tailor's shop in Massachusetts, he was transported back to New Haven Superior Court, where he was found guilty of his third burglary offense and sentenced to be hanged. While being held for execution, he escaped. Embarrassed by the escape, the New Haven jailhouse keeper, who had sworn he would be able to hold the notorious escape artist, offered a $20 reward for Frasier's capture. A local newspaper published a story with Frasier's description in it and the announcement of the reward. Frasier was described as "of middling Stature, black Hair, pitted with the Small-Pox, has both his Ears cropped, and branded twice on his Forehead with the Capital Letter B, his Fore-Teeth gone, aged about Twenty-Eight Years; had on a brown Great Coat, a Pair of old Homespun Breeches, and a Check Shirt."

Frasier fled Connecticut and headed back to Massachusetts but was once again apprehended and sent back to New Haven to await execution. While incarcerated, this time under heavy guard, he petitioned the Connecticut state legislature for clemency, with the help of an attorney, on the grounds that the severity of the punishment of hanging did not fit the nature of the crimes of petty thefts and burglary. Through his attorney he argued that, without leniency by the legislature, he would become the first person to be executed in Connecticut for the third offense of mere burglary. His appeal fell on deaf ears. No reprieve was forthcoming.

The stairway to the scaffold during the colonial period in America was comparatively unsystematic. From colony to colony, the punishment meted out varied, although the overall colonial judicial system had in place a series of punishments that increased in severity for repeat offenders like Frasier. The usual punishment for crimes against property included public whipping, branding or ear cropping, fines, and servitude to pay off the courts and victims. The various colonies developed a majority of their penal codes from English rule. The crimes of treason, murder, manslaughter, arson, rape, and witchcraft were considered capital offenses punishable by hanging. Under some colonial laws, certain types of burglary were punishable by death (in Massachusetts most notably), but in most regions of New England, it did not reach the level of a capital offense until after the third conviction. Hence, even as far back as colonial times, the three strikes rule in criminal offenses was maintained.

Prior to his execution, Frasier wrote *A Brief Account of the Life, and Abominable Thefts, of the Notorious Isaac Frasier*. In it, he related his brief life of crime throughout New England and New York and confessed to more than fifty counts of burglary that he could recall. Unable to read or write, Frasier dictated the account and signed it by marking an X for his name. In one account, Frasier said he "stole a Goose from Mr. Samuel Jennison, and from the Widow Kingsley. In the same Place, we stole a Kettle, in which we boiled the Goose."

According to Frasier, in order to avoid prosecution, he often took advantage of making private settlements with his victims. In his *A Brief Account*, he spelled out in some detail instances where he eluded prosecution by making amends financially or otherwise with the victims he stole from. In Providence, Frasier stole someone's hat but escaped prosecution by settling up with the owner by returning it, remarking that it never fit him correctly. But even when he was caught for his nefarious deeds by the authorities, Frasier, managed to escape. The jails that did exist lacked adequate security and were poorly constructed. Frasier admitted to numerous jailbreaks, including breaking out of jails in Newport, Rhode Island; Litchfield, Fairfield and New Haven, Connecticut; and Cambridge and Worcester, Massachusetts. After breaking into a shop in Fairfield, Connecticut, in March 1768, Frasier stole a horse in order to make his getaway but was caught. He was thrown into the Fairfield jail to await trial.

Newly built, the jail was hailed as one of the strongest and safest in the New England colonies. Still, it couldn't hold him. Locked up in a cell, Frasier connived with a prisoner being held in the cell next to him to escape. The jail mate provided Frasier with some embers from the stove that was burning next to his cell and Frasier used the embers to burn a hole in the wall in order to escape. The flames raged out of control and the entire jail caught fire. Luckily, Frasier and the other prisoner were rescued, but the fire couldn't be contained. The jail, the new courthouse next door, and two other buildings caught fire and were burned to the ground. Although Frasier was not charged with the arson, he was transferred to another jail to await trial. Although he was developing a reputation as an incompetent thief, his status as an escape artist grew exponentially, which, more than anything else, galled the authorities. Besides confessing to his many crimes in *A Brief Account*, Frasier credited the start of his life of crime to his lack of any formal education and his abuse as a child while serving as a shoemaker's apprentice. He implored parents to teach their children and to be careful of the type of character they have their children apprentice with. Teaching virtue and religion to children was essential to avoid the end he now faced.

On September 7, 1768, twenty-eight-year-old Isaac Frasier, the "Notorious Frasier," was led to the gallows in Fairfield, Connecticut. The irony of Frasier's execution, according to historian Daniel Cohen, that it was more likely Frasier's notoriety—"The Notorious Frasier"—and his repeated escapes from jail that embarrassed the authorities that led to his execution, not his litany of petty crimes and burglaries.

A huge crowd gathered for the hanging. Frasier chose not to give any last words but asked that the town minister, Reverend Noah Hobart, give a sermon. In his sermon, titled "Excessive Wickedness, the Way to an untimely Death," Hobart claimed, "Men go from one degree of wickedness to another. . . . Justice requires that you should suffer." He ended the sermon pleading with Frasier to accept salvation.

Capital punishment had been on the books in Connecticut since 1642. Third-time offenders faced the death penalty in Connecticut, as in many of the colonies; however, Frasier became the first burglar—by and large a petty thief—to be hanged for his crimes. Several weeks after Frasier's execution, a Hartford, Connecticut, newspaper published an article titled "An Answer to a Very Important Question, Whether Any Community Has a Right to Punish Any Species of Theft with Death?" The unnamed writer's answer was a categorical NO! Much of the argument in the article was based on the discourse "On Crimes and Punishments," written by the Italian nobleman Cesare Beccaria, originally published in Italian in 1764 and in America in 1767. In his treatise, Beccaria argued that although punishment must be swift and certain in their nature, they did not necessarily have to be severe in order to be effective. Beccaria further maintained that capital punishment did not deter crime. He argued that punishment should be in proportion to the crime and the crimes should be weighed in terms of their severity on society. He said that the history of the death penalty had not prevented crime and that it was merely a "momentary spectacle, and therefore a less efficacious method of deterring others, than the continued example of a man deprived of his liberty."

"If we glance at the pages of history, we will find that laws, which surely are, or ought to be, compacts of free men, have been, for the most part, a mere tool for the passions of some," Beccaria wrote.

The outcry that followed the execution of the uneducated, abused, and branded Isaac Frasier was the beginning of the movement to abolish the death penalty in America, except for the most heinous of crimes. The first attempt to reform the death penalty in America occurred when Thomas Jefferson introduced a bill in 1777 to revise Virginia's death penalty laws. The bill proposed that capital punishment be used only for the crimes of murder and treason. It was defeated by a single vote. Still, the floodgates had been opened on the use of the death penalty in America as a deterrent on crime. Dr. Benjamin Rush, a signer of the *Declaration of Independence*, argued that having a death penalty actually increased crime. One of Rush's supporters, Philadelphia attorney general William Bradford, led Pennsylvania to become the first state to consider degrees of murder based on culpability. And in 1794, Pennsylvania repealed the death penalty for all offenses except first-degree murder. America has come a long way since it executed people like Isaac Frasier for petty thefts and burglaries, but has it come far enough?

The State of Connecticut voted to abolish the death penalty in April 2012. Of the major industrialized nations, the United States remains one of the few that still executes criminals.

Last Wednesday evening the notorious FRASIER, who was under sentence of death for burglary, as has been mentioned, was brought from Worcester, (where he was taken up for theft, and whipt) and recommitted to the goal [sic] in this town, from whence he escaped about a month since,—in which time he has committed five or six burglaries and thefts, and traveled near 500 miles. The next night but one after his escape, he broke open no less than three shops in Middletown, from one of which he stole 70l value in goods and cash. The Superior Court now sitting in Fairfield, have given strict orders, that he should be loaded with chains, and the goal guarded every night till the time of his execution.

—*THE CONNECTICUT GAZETTE*, SEPTEMBER 2, 1768

CHAPTER 3

The Strawberry Basket Murder

Hannah Ocuish, 1786

GOD admonishing his People of their Duty,
as Parents and Masters.

A
S E R M O N,

PREACHED AT

N E W - L O N D O N,
December 20th, 1786.

OCCASIONED
By the EXECUTION
Of *Hannah Ocuish,* a Mulatto Girl,
Aged 12 Years and 9 Months.

For the M U R D E R
of *EUNICE BOLLES,*
Aged 6 Years and 6 Months.

By HNRY CHANNING, M. A.

THE SECOND EDITION.

to himself, bringeth his Mother to shame.
WISDOM.
If I did despise the cause of my Man-servant, or of my Maid-
servant, when they contended with me : what then shall I do
when God riseth up ? and when he visiteth, what shall I an-
swer ?....Did not he that made me in the womb, make him ?
JOB.

N E W - L O N D O N:
Printed by T. GREEN. M,DCC,LXXXVI.

Hannah Ocuish, a twelve-year-old Pequot Indian girl, was hung, making her the youngest female juvenile executed in the country.

When twelve-year-old Hannah Ocuish was hung for murder on December 20, 1786 in New London, Connecticut, she became the youngest female juvenile executed in the country, all because of a basket of strawberries.

IN LATE JUNE 1786, THE STRAWBERRY FIELDS IN NEW LONDON, Connecticut, were filled with ripe strawberries and dozens of children ran through the fields gathering strawberries in their baskets. Six-year-old Eunice Bolles was among them. She was the daughter of a wealthy New London farmer. She had picked a small basket of strawberries and left the basket lying on the ground. When she returned to get it, all the strawberries she'd so carefully picked were gone. Hannah Ocuish, a twelve-year-old orphan, who was working in servitude for a widow at a nearby farm, had emptied Bolles's basket into her own.

Bolles reportedly began to cry and threatened to tell one of the adults what Ocuish had done—stolen her strawberries. Ocuish was big for her age and known among the other children as a bully. She tried to silence the crying girl by threatening to beat her if she didn't keep quiet, but Bolles wouldn't be intimidated by the older girl and would not let the matter go. Instead, she told one of the adults what Ocuish had done and Ocuish was forced to give back the strawberries she had taken and was banished from the strawberry field. Ocuish swore revenge but she was in no hurry, waiting patiently instead for the right time to inflict her revenge. It came five months later.

Ocuish was born in 1774 in Groton, Connecticut. She was a Pequot Indian girl with an intellectual disability. She had an older brother. Her mother, a full-blooded Pequot Indian, was an alcoholic who often disappeared from the family for months at a time. Her father was a white man but had long ago abandoned his wife and family. Ocuish was only six years old when she had her first brush with the law. She and her older brother held up a small girl and beat her brutally, ripped her clothes, and stole her small gold locket from her. The young victim managed to escape and ran home. Ocuish and her brother were quickly apprehended. As a result of the robbery, Hannah and her brother were removed from their mother's custody and turned over to different homes where they were placed in bound servitude, a standard practice at the time. Her brother was never seen again. By 1786, she was working for a widow at a small farm just outside New London, Connecticut. There had been no further incidents, but Ocuish was known as a tyrant among the other children and they stayed clear of her.

On July 21, 1786, while she was out filling a water bucket for her mistress, Ocuish saw Bolles walking alone up a deserted road on her way to school. She put down the water bucket and grabbed a small piece of calico cloth. She chased after Bolles calling her name. She sprinted down the road and jumped over a nearby stone wall to confront the smaller girl.

Ocuish pretended to forgive and forget what had transpired with the basket of strawberries the past summer and offered the little girl a token gift, the swatch of calico cloth. Bolles was pleasantly surprised by Ocuish's friendly behavior. She reached out and took the calico cloth that Ocuish held out for her. Her eyes were glued to the colorful cloth, otherwise she might have seen what Ocuish held in her other hand—a rock.

Ocuish struck Bolles in the head with the rock with a tremendous blow, stunning the small girl. Bolles cried out but it was too late and there was none around to hear her screams. In a state of raging fury, Ocuish continued to repeatedly hit the girl in the head. Bolles lay on the ground, a bloody mess. Her head and body were badly mangled and both her back and one arm were broken. But Bolles still wasn't dead. She began to stir. Ocuish decided to finish the job. She grabbed the little girl by the throat and choked the life out of her. Then, to cover up the murder, she piled rocks from the nearby stone wall atop the body to make it appear that Bolles had met with an accident scaling the stone wall. Ocuish fled the scene.

A passerby discovered the body a few hours later. As a nearby resident, Ocuish was one of the first people questioned. She had a story all prepared. She told the authorities that she had noticed something unusual that morning. She said she saw four boys trespassing in the widow's garden. She said she chased them away and they ran down the road along the stone wall. Not too long afterwards, she said, she heard a strange sound, like the noise of stones falling from a fence. The neighbors investigating the crime believed otherwise. Bolles's death was not caused by a falling stone wall. The finger marks on her throat ruled out the possibility of an accident. Ocuish became the prime suspect.

According to reports, "On the 21st of July, 1786, at about 10 o'clock in the morning, the body of the murdered child was found in the public road leading from New London to Norwich, lying on its face near to a wall." Bolles's body displayed signs of extreme trauma. "The head and body were mangled in a shocking manner, the back and one arm broken, and a number of heavy stones placed on the body, arms and legs."

The neighborhood turned out to hunt for the murderer. In 1786, before the professionalization of law enforcement in the country, investigators of Bolles's murder were local townspeople. Investigators questioned Ocuish, who initially denied any involvement, but told them the story she had made up about the four boys she had seen. A search failed to turn the boys up. Investigators began to doubt the girl's story.

On July 22, "she was closely questioned, but repeatedly denied that she was guilty." Still unconvinced, the investigators took Ocuish to the house where Bolles's body was. Confronted with Bolles's bloody, battered body she broke down and confessed and told them everything, from the strawberries to the stones.

According to an anonymous report, investigators "carried [Hannah] to the house where the body lay, and being charged with the crime, burst into tears and confessed that she killed her, saying if she could be forgiven, she would never do so again."

Hannah's confession, which was accepted as truth by the court, indicated that she had sought revenge because Bolles had "complained of her in strawberry time . . . for taking away her strawberries." The primary evidence against her was her confession. She was placed on trial for murder.

According to an anonymous report of her trial in October, Ocuish, "appeared entirely unconcerned."

"Theft and lying were her common vices. To these were added a maliciousness of disposition which made the children in the neighborhood much afraid of her. She had a degree of artful cunning and sagacity beyond many of her years," the unnamed author of the report wrote.

Because of Ocuish mental disability, it was questioned whether she was fit to stand trial at all, but the judge at the trial indicated he saw value in using her conviction to send a message to the local community. Finding her guilty based on her confession, he sentenced her to be hanged. Reports described Ocuish as seemingly unconcerned by her death sentence.

The trial was one of the most bizarre spectacles to grace a colonial courtroom. There was no juvenile court and children were tried as adults. Still, some found the sight of a twelve-year-old girl on trial for her life disturbing. Various anonymous accounts of the trial describe emotions "running high in the audience." Even the judge was reported often near tears. The calmest person in the courtroom was Ocuish, who appeared unconcerned throughout the proceedings. Many suspected that, because of her limited mental capabilities, she did not fully understand the severity of her crime or the trial. The judge may have been sympathetic to the case, but he managed to keep any hint of sentimentality out of his final decision.

In reviewing the evidence, he found elements of malice, premeditation, and obstruction. In sentencing her, he said:

> You must consider and realize it, that after death you must undergo another trial infinitely more solemn and awful than what you have passed through, before that God against whom you offended—at whose bar the deceased child will appear as a swift witness against you . . . the sparing of you, on account of your age, would . . . be of dangerous consequences to the public, by holding up an idea that children might commit such atrocious acts with impunity.

He sentenced her to be hung by the neck until dead. But even the death sentence didn't appear to phase Ocuish. Locked in her cell, she appeared to be carefree. She didn't have to work, received lots of attention, and could even play with the children who came to visit her there. One observer said that she "frequently would make very shrewd turns upon those persons who made severe remarks upon her."

Reality sank in about two weeks before the hanging when she realized that there would be no reprieve. She became inconsolable. On December 20, less than five months after the murder of Eunice Bolles, she was taken from her cell and marched out before a crowd that had gathered behind the New London meetinghouse. The Sheriff of New London led the distraught girl to the gallows, placed a rope around her neck, and hanged her in front of the crowd of spectators. She thanked the sheriff for his kindness as she stepped forward to be hanged. At twelve years old, Ocuish was the youngest female offender executed by any state. Her death remains the last documented execution of a female in the State of Connecticut.

Reverend Henry Channing of Yale preached at her execution and published his sermon under the title, "God Admonishing His People of Their Duty . . . a Sermon . . . Occasioned by the Execution of Hannah Ocuish, a Mulatto Girl, Aged 12 Years and 9 Months, for the Murder of Eunice Bolles, Aged 6 Years and 6 Months." The sermon admonished parents not to neglect religious instruction for their children. Ocuish's crimes, he argued, were the "natural consequences of too great parental indulgence," and warned that "appetites and passions unrestrained in childhood become furious in youth; and ensure dishonor, disease and an untimely death."

In the United States, the youngest children put to death by the government have all been children of color. James Arcene, a Cherokee boy, was only ten or eleven years old when he was tried for committing a robbery and murder that resulted in his 1885 hanging in Arkansas. In the twentieth century, the youngest children executed were both African American: thirteen-year-old Fortune Ferguson of Florida (1927) and fourteen-year-old George Stinney of South Carolina (1944). In 2005, the US Supreme Court abolished the death penalty for criminals who committed their crimes as juveniles. The ruling was based on *Roper v. Simmons*. In Missouri, in 1993, seventeen-year-old Christopher Simmons murdered Shirley Nite Crook. At trial, the jury returned a guilty verdict and recommended the death sentence. The case was appealed to the US Supreme Court. *Roper v. Simmons* was a landmark decision in which the Supreme Court held that it is unconstitutional to impose capital punishment for crimes committed while under the age of eighteen.

HANNAH!—prisoner at the bar—agreeably to the laws of the land you have arraigned, tried and convicted of the crime of murder. . . .

The good and safety of society requires, that no one, of such a malignant character, shall be suffered to live, and the punishment of death is but the just demerit of your crime: and the sparing you on account of your age, would, as the law says, be of dangerous consequence to the publick, by holding up an idea, that children might commit such atrocious crimes with impunity. . . . And you must consider that after death you must undergo another trial, infinitely more solemn and awful than what you have here passed through, before that God against whom you offended; at whose bar the deceased child will appear as a swift witness against you—And you will be condemned and consigned to an everlasting punishment, unless you now obtain a pardon, by confessing and sincerely repenting of your sins, and applying to his sovereign grace, through the merits of his Son, Jesus Christ, for mercy, who is able and willing to save the greatest offenders, who repent and believe in him.

—REVEREND HENRY CHANNING, "GOD ADMONISHING HIS PEOPLE OF THEIR DUTY, AS PARENTS AND MASTERS," DECEMBER 20, 1786.

CHAPTER 4

Stick'em Up

Patrick Lyon, 1798

PATRICK LYON,

who suffered three months severe imprisonment on merely a vague suspicion for the internal Robbery of the Bank of Pennsylvania.

Patrick Lyon, a blacksmith, was arrested and imprisoned for the first recorded bank robbery in America in 1798.

In 1798, Patrick Lyon, a Philadelphia-based blacksmith, was arrested and thrown in jail, charged with committing the first recorded bank robbery in America, but Lyon was ultimately able to clear his name and win a substantial financial judgment against those who wrongly imprisoned him.

Sometime during the night of August 31 or the early morning of September 1, 1798, the Bank of Pennsylvania, located in Carpenters' Hall in Philadelphia, was robbed of $162,821, roughly $1.9 million based on today's monetary standard. It was the first recorded bank robbery in America.

There was no sign of forced entry reported either into the building where the money was being kept or the vault where it was stored. There were no visible signs of damage to the Hall doors or locks. The robber or robbers, whichever the case might have been, simply unlocked the doors to the Hall and the locks on the vault and stole the money, leading the authorities to surmise it had been an inside job. The question remained—who on the inside had done it?

City magistrate and bank director, John C. Stocker, decided the culprit must have been Patrick Lyon, a local blacksmith, who had been hired to refit locks on the doors at the bank. According to Stocker's theory, Lyons must have made an extra key to let himself in after dark and stole the money. Lyon, who had left the city, turned himself into authorities to clear his good name.

The Bank of Pennsylvania had made plans during the summer of 1798 to move its base of operations to Carpenters' Hall on Chestnut Street. The historic Carpenters' Hall was an elegant brick Georgian building and the site of the historic First Continental Congress in 1774. The building also housed Franklin's Library Company, the American colony's first lending library begun by Benjamin Franklin and the American Philosophical Society. The American Philosophical Society is the oldest learned society in the United States, founded in 1743 by Benjamin Franklin and many founders of the country were members, including George Washington, John Adams, Thomas Jefferson, Alexander Hamilton, James Madison, and John Marshall. It was into these hallowed halls that the Bank of

Pennsylvania moved in the summer of 1798. The Hall had proved itself to be a safe temporary location for two other notable banks, including Robert Morris' Bank of North America and Alexander Hamilton's First Bank of the United States.

Samuel Robinson, a member of the Carpenters' Hall guild, was placed in charge of the bank's move. Robinson decided that the iron vault doors for the bank required new locks and took them to Patrick Lyon's blacksmith shop. Lyon was a well-known and reputable blacksmith and locksmith. It was said that he could open up the most difficult lock in a matter of minutes. Born in London in 1779, Lyon began his apprenticeship at the age of ten years old. He immigrated to America in 1793, settling in Philadelphia.

Although Lyon was contacted by Robinson to change locks and fittings on two iron doors, which were brought to his shop, he informed Robinson that the doors were not proper for a bank and the locks were insecure. Robinson disregarded Lyon's advice and explained that there was a great need to hurry to fix the locks. Lyon did as he was told. While the doors were in Lyon's shop being fitted, Robinson and a man named Isaac Davis came to inspect them. On Monday, August 14, the refitted doors with their new locks were hung at Carpenters' Hall. Still, Lyon insisted that neither the doors nor the locks were sufficient to protect the bank's holdings. Once more Robinson rebuffed him. As far as Lyon was concerned, that was the end of it. He couldn't have been more wrong.

In the late summer of 1798, yellow fever was spreading through Philadelphia, the largest city in America. It appeared likely that the illness, which was spread by mosquito bites, was transported by the crews and passengers from the multitude of ships anchored in the Philadelphia port along the Delaware and Schuylkill Rivers. Five years earlier in 1793, the largest yellow fever epidemic in the country hit Philadelphia killing approximately 5,000 inhabitants. At the time of both epidemics, doctors did not know the role mosquitoes played in the spread of the disease.

When the second outbreak of the fever hit Philadelphia in 1798, many inhabitants decided to flee. Lyon was among them. Sadly, he had already lost his wife and child to the plague. Ultimately, approximately 1,300 people would die in the epidemic. Lyon was not to be one of them and he hoped neither would his nineteen-year-old apprentice, James M'Ginley. They booked passage aboard a small ship heading to Cape Henlopen, but by the time they disembarked at Lewistown, Delaware, M'Ginley was sick. Despite his best efforts and the help of several physicians, M'Ginley died.

Following the death and burial of his apprentice in Lewistown, Lyon signed on to a variety of odd jobs to make ends meet while he waited out the yellow fever epidemic in Philadelphia. What he didn't know at the time was that he had become a prime suspect in the Bank of Pennsylvania robbery and it was only by happenstance that he learned of it. Lawmen and a citizen posse were combing New Jersey for him, including the Philadelphia high constable John Haines. There was a $2,000 reward out for Lyon's capture.

Most of the talk in Lewistown, where Lyon was staying, was about the yellow fever epidemic in Philadelphia, but eventually word arrived about the bank robbery. Lyon was keenly interested in the newspaper accounts of the robbery, since the last job he had was at the bank. According to the reports, the robbery was an inside job, since there was no sign of forced entry into the building or the bank vault. Lyon immediately suspected Robinson, the man who had hired him, and the stranger, Isaac Davis, Robinson had brought with him to his blacksmith shop to inspect his work. When he learned he was a prime suspect in the robbery, he returned to Philadelphia.

Lyon walked from Brandywine to Philadelphia, a distance of 150 miles, intent on clearing his name and making known his own suspicions about Samuel Robinson and Isaac Davis. He arrived in Philadelphia on September 21. When he turned himself in and passed on his suspicions about Robinson and Davis, he wasn't believed.

Lyon was interrogated by Samuel M. Fox, president of the Bank of Pennsylvania; Jonathan Smith, the head cashier; John C. Stocker, one of the directors of bank; and also one of the Philadelphia aldermen and Philadelphia High Constable John Haines. His interrogators found his story about leaving the city so soon after the robbery to be contrived. The authorities suspected Lyon had made an extra key when working on the new locks and it was by using the extra key that he was able to break into

Carpenters' Hall and the bank without leaving any trace. They officially charged Lyon and committed him to the Walnut Street Prison with an incredibly high bail $150,000, which Lyon could never have met. Even after walking some 150 miles to turn himself in, professing his innocence, and providing authorities with information about the possible real culprits in the robbery, he was locked up and spent three harrowing months in the Walnut Street Prison.

In his 1799 memoir, printed as a pamphlet, with the preposterous title of *Narrative of Patrick Lyon Who Suffered Three Months Severe Imprisonment in Philadelphia Gaol on Merely a Vague Suspicion of Being Concerned in a Robbery of the Bank of Pennsylvania with His Remarks Thereon*, Lyon wrote, "I found I was in the hands of those who are not the most intelligent of mankind."

Yellow fever was spreading inside the stone walls of the prison and Lyon feared he would not survive. In his memoir, Lyon described his twelve-foot-by-four-foot prison cell as, "cold, damp, unwholesome and solitary." He did manage to survive a bout of yellow fever and kept busy in lockup by reading, writing, and praying. He entered the prison with copy of the Bible and a collection of Robert Burns's *Poems*. Given a quill pen, paper, and ink, he began writing his memoir. He lost weight, grew a long beard and hair, and, despite being abandoned by previous friends, he remained steadfast in his innocence.

While Lyon was languishing in prison, the real culprit, Isaac Davis, the stranger who had accompanied Samuel Robinson to Lyon's shop to inspect the refitted locks, remained free, but not for very long. Davis came from one of Philadelphia's most influential and well-respected families. His uncle, Benjamin Brannon, was an associate judge of Delaware County. But regardless of his lineage, Isaac Davis was considered a dimwit.

In truth, Davis and a bank employee named Thomas Cunningham had pulled off the heist. Cunningham hid inside the bank after it closed and let Davis in that night. Davis claimed it was Cunningham who had duplicate keys made for the vault locks, although he did not know where or how Cunningham had obtained them. They easily unlocked the vault with the copy of the vault key that Lyon had made for him and the two men easily slipped away with the money. It would have gone off perfectly if Cunningham, who appeared to have been the brains behind the robbery, hadn't succumbed to the yellow fever that was raging through the city. Cunningham died shortly after the robbery, never having an opportunity to enjoy his share of the stolen loot.

The dim-witted Davis, surely a pawn in Cunningham's plot, was then left to his own devices and his actions were at best criminally naive and at worst just plain stupid. In order to hide the money from the robbery, Davis began depositing the stolen loot in banks throughout the city, including in the very bank he had robbed it from, the Bank of Pennsylvania at Carpenters' Hall. Bank authorities took note of Davis's newfound wealth demonstrated in his deposits to several banks throughout the city and confronted him.

Confronted with questions about his newfound wealth, Davis broke down and gave a full confession and made a deal to return all the money. He told authorities that Patrick Lyon had no involvement in the heist and also wrote a letter to Lyon declaring him innocent of any knowledge of the crime. Given Davis's standing in the community, the governor of Pennsylvania promised a pardon in return for full disclosure and full restitution. Davis agreed to return all the money in exchange for a full pardon. He ultimately returned all but $2,000 of the missing loot and, although he never spent a day in jail, he was banished from the city.

According to court testimony, "On the 20th of November it was published in the newspapers, that Isaac Davis was the robber, and nearly the whole of the money was found upon him. Isaac Davis, by threats and promises confessed that he and one Cunningham, a porter to the bank who died in Philadelphia of the yellow fever, were the only two persons concerned in the robbery."

Despite the full confession by Davis, the return of the money, and his letter indicating that Patrick Lyon had no involvement in the heist, the authorities, both bank and law officers, stubbornly insisted that Lyon was still a suspect in the case, accusing him of being the person who made the duplicate keys for Davis and Cunningham. Lyon suffered in jail for several more weeks. The directors of the bank did not want to face their culpability in the wrongful arrest and imprisonment of Lyon, and they refused to set Lyon free, insisting that he was an accessory to the crime.

With everything that had happened with Davis, it became impossible for authorities to continue to hold Lyon. The charges against him were dismissed and his good name was cleared by a grand jury in January 1799. Still, even after his release from prison and the publication of his memoir in that same year, Lyon lived several years in poverty, shunned by his former friends and business associates. He was determined to get redress to his wrongful imprisonment and resolved to get vindication through civil action in the courts.

In 1805, he filed a civil case against the Bank President Samuel Fox; Head Cashier Jonathan Smith; Alderman and Bank Board Member John Stocker and Constable John Haines. An all-star cast of prominent lawyers represented the two sides. The defendants hired signers of the US Constitution, Attorney Jared Ingersoll and William Rawle. Lyon's attorneys included Alexander J. Dallas, a distinguished lawyer who was later appointed US Secretary of the Treasury by President James Madison and Joseph Hopkinson, and considered to be one the country's most skilled lawyers. He was the son of another signer of the Declaration of Independence, Francis Hopkinson. About two dozen witnesses were called. It was up to Lyon's legal team to prove that bank and law enforcement officials acted with premeditated malice.

According to testimony in the case, reported in the 1808, *Robbery of the Bank of Pennsylvania in 1798: The Trial in the Supreme Court*, Hopkinson told the jury. "Instead of discharging Lyon, and compensating him for his sufferings, they went on with a prosecution against him, not for robbery, but as an accomplice. The bill of indictment was presented two months after all was discovered, yet notwithstanding Lyon was continued in prison."

Pennsylvania associate supreme court justice Jasper Yeates [Yates], sitting on the civil case, told the jury that it must rule on the question of malice, which hinged on probable cause to arrest and detain Lyon. If there was probable cause, the judge said then there was no malice.

Yeates also told the jury, "It is of importance to the community, that where offences are committed, the offender should be punished, and this without regard to persons; everyone is interested in the common cause, the rich and the poor, the master and the servant are equally affected."

The jury retired at 4:30 p.m. and made up their verdict at 8 p.m. The next morning, the jury returned with a whopping $12,000 verdict in favor of Lyon. According to the trial records,

> *The moment the verdict was delivered by the foreman of the jury, a universal clamor of exultation took place among the audience, the most numerous the reporter remembers ever to have assembled in that court room. Justice Yates ordered silence, and told the citizens applauding, that they were not in a playhouse, but of justice.*

The defendants appealed and were granted a new trial set to begin in March 1807, but just as the new trial was about to begin, the two parties settled out of court and an agreement was reached awarding Lyon $9,000. It was a large amount, equal to several years' wages for any working man like Lyon. Aside from the money, Lyon's name was finally cleared. He would no longer be associated with the first bank robbery in America, at least not as the perpetrator of the crime.

"Pat Lyon at the Forge," an oil on canvas portrait was painted by John Neagle in 1829 and hangs in the Pennsylvania Academy of Fine Arts, in Philadelphia, a gift from the Lyon Family. The portrait depicts a young apprentice working at the bellows in the background of Lyon's blacksmith shop. It was a unique unusual portrait for the time because it showed Lyon wearing his leather apron, hammer in hand, pounding at his anvil. During this period, people with enough money to commission a portrait usually did so posed in formal attire depicting their lofty social status. Despite the blacksmith location, Lyon managed to have his newfound wealth and community status shown by the billowing white shirt he wore in the painting and the very formal and dressy silver buckle shoes he wore in the portrait. As if as a reminder of where he had come from, in the upper-left-hand corner in the portrait, Neagle painted the cupola and weather-vane atop the Walnut Street Prison.

Lyon had been prosecuted by bank and law enforcement authorities because of his low status as an immigrant craftsman, but following his civil case judgment, he was no longer seen as a symbol of America's working class. In the years following the civil case, Lyon became a businessman, a landlord, and manufacturer of fire engines.

> *It is an observation I long have made, that the great when they have power, will often make a wrong use of it, and that those who are inferior in rank, have very little chance of justice when opposed to them; as riches furnish a variety of means both to elude and oppose, the effective force of the law. Though everyone ought to have his full portion of justice, yet I believe no one will doubt, that it is not generally the case; the rich can elude justice by giving great bail, and feeing lawyers high, who by that and other methods, protract the affair till the action dies away by one means or another; there is nothing incomprehensible in all this—If the small fry get in the least entramelled in the meshes of the law, they are generally fastened in the net, and often times punished wrongfully. For as Hudibras observes, For justice though it punish crimes, Stumbles on the innocent sometimes.*
>
> —PATRICK LYON, *THE NARRATIVE OF PATRICK LYON, WHO SUFFERED THREE MONTHS SEVERE IMPRISONMENT IN PHILADELPHIA GAOL; ON MERELY A VAGUE SUSPICION, OF BEING CONCERNED IN THE ROBBERY OF THE BANK OF PENNSYLVANIA,* 1829.

CHAPTER 5

The Factory Girl's Murder

Ephraim Avery, 1832

In 1832, Methodist minister Ephraim Avery murdered Sarah Cornell, an unmarried, pregnant factory worker, to conceal his involvement with her.

When twenty-nine-year-old Sarah Maria Cornell, an unmarried, pregnant factory worker hung herself in Tiverton, Rhode Island, in 1832, the authorities immediately concluded the girl had committed suicide to hide her shame, but letters found in the dead girl's possession pointed to something far more sinister.

On Friday, December 21, 1832, the body of a young woman was discovered hanging from a length of rope tied to beam in a barn on the farm of John Durfee in the town of Tiverton, Rhode Island. The farm was just across the border from Fall River, Massachusetts. Durfee cut her frozen lifeless body down and covered it with a cloak but did not recognize the girl nor did he understand why she had chosen to hang herself on his farm.

He immediately sent for the coroner. When the news reached nearby Fall River, Ira Bidwell, a local Methodist minister; John Smith, the boss of the Fall River Manufactory, a weaving mill; and Dr. Thomas Wilbur, a local physician, all arrived at the farm. Reverend Bidwell recognized the girl as Sarah Maria Cornell, a member of his Fall River congregation. When initially asked if he recognized her, Bidwell said, "Yes I know her. She is a respectable young woman, and a member of my church." He would change his tune very shortly.

John Smith verified her identity stating that she worked in the weaving room of his factory. Dr. Wilbur also identified the body as one of his patients. Whatever the doctor initially thought regarding her death, he kept it to himself until an inquest could be held. Although everyone in their immediate haste concluded the poor girl had committed suicide, Dr. Wilbur was privy to information that would prove otherwise.

Durfee had the girl's body taken to his house. He inquired of Bidwell if the young woman had any friends or family who could be called on and whether his congregation would pay for her burial. Bidwell said he would consult with the elders of his congregation and get back to him. Before he could leave, Dr. Wilbur, who had been struggling with the knowledge about the dead girl that he possessed, took Bidwell aside. He informed the minister that Cornell had recently confessed to him that she was pregnant with the child of a married Methodist minister named Ephraim Avery.

Wilbur told Bidwell that he had met with Cornell in October and that the young woman had revealed everything to him. Bidwell's reaction to the shocking news was defensive. He defended Avery claiming he was a good and pious man and was perfectly innocent of any charges the Cornell girl might have levied against him. What was even more dramatic was Bidwell's complete turnaround regarding the character of Cornell. Although he had initially stated to Durfee and others that Cornell was a "respectable young woman," he blurted out that "the deceased was a very bad character, and that Avery had told him so, and warned him against her, and that she was not in full communion with the meeting but only received upon probation." Both Wilbur and Durfee were shocked. Wilbur confided in Bidwell that the girl had probably committed suicide out of despair.

Bidwell left and returned later to inform Durfee and Wilbur that because of Cornell's "bad character," his congregation "would have nothing to do with burying her." Durfee, a hardworking, honest man, proclaimed that he would not deny a proper burial to the young woman, regardless of Bidwell's proclamation.

"She shall have a burial place in my grounds," Durfee said, "near my family, and as respectable a funeral as anybody, and as respectable a clergyman as any other to make the prayer, and everything that is necessary and decent shall be attended to."

Preparations for her burial were begun, but first an ad hoc coroner's jury was convened. The jury at first agreed with Dr. Wilbur's assessment that the poor girl had hanged herself in a fit of despair. They declared her death a suicide and she was buried that Saturday. Several women from the town prepared the body for burial. While they were preparing the body, Durfee and several others went to the house in Fall River where Cornell had lived to find some suitable clothes for the burial and to see if they could find the names of relatives or friends who should be contacted.

Looking through Cornell's small apartment, Durfee found a trunk. Inside it were four letters. One letter was addressed to Reverend Bidwell. The other three letters had been sent to Cornell anonymously. One of the women who had accompanied Durfee to Cornell's apartment found a small strip of paper and written in pencil on it were the words—"If I am missing enquire of the Rev. E. K. Avery." It was signed by Cornell. Since the funeral was scheduled to begin shortly, the letters and strip of paper were gathered up, but it would not be until the next day that anyone would examine them closely.

Examination of the letters turned the world upside down. That Saturday, a small crowd gathered at Durfee's farmhouse, and Reverend James Fowler, a Congregational minister, gave a brief prayer service. The body of Sarah Maria Cornell was taken from the farmhouse to her place of burial on the Durfee Family plot, only to be exhumed the next day as more evidence based on the four letters came to light.

According to Dr. Wilbur's assessment the day after the burial, Cornell's death mask was not one of suicide. "That look never was seen on the countenance of a person who did not die by violence," Wilbur said.

After the body was exhumed, a jury inquest was held. Three physicians examined the body. It was confirmed that she was pregnant at the time of her death. Bruises on her abdomen suggested that an abortion of some sort might have been attempted. Further examination of the body showed that she could not have died from hanging since the rope found around her neck used a clove hitch—the knot requiring that both ends of it had to be drawn tight to cause suffocation, and therefore she could not have hung herself. The jury concluded that Cornell had been strangled with the rope before she was suspended from the beam inside Durfee's barn. All the new physical evidence pointed to murder and the four letters found in Cornell's apartment pointed directly to the killer—Reverend Ephraim Avery.

The four letters and scrap of paper found in Cornell's trunk were carefully examined. Three of the letters—one yellow, one pink, and one white—were addressed to Cornell. One letter was written by Cornell to the Reverend Bidwell and the scrap of paper written in pencil was the most damning of all the evidence found that pointed to Avery as the murder suspect. The scrap of paper simply read: "If I should be missing, enquire of the Rev. Mr. Avery in Bristol. He will know where I am gone." It was dated December 20, 1832, and signed S. M. Cornell.

The letter that Cornell wrote to Bidwell stated:

I take this opportunity to inform you that for reasons known to God and my own soul I wish no longer to be connected with the Methodist Society. When I came to this place I thought I should enjoy myself among them but as I do not enjoy any Religion attall [sic], I have not seen a well nor a happy day since I left Thompson campground. You will therefore please to drop my name from [the Bible Class], and I will try to gain all the instruction I can from your public labors. I hope I shall feel different some time or other. The Methodists are my people when I enjoy any Religion. To them I was Indebted under God for my spiritual birth. I once knew what it was to love God with all my heart once felt God was my father, Jesus my friend and Heaven my home but have awfully departed and sometimes feel I shall lose my soul forever. I desire your prayer that God would help me from this.

It was signed, "Yours respectfully, Sarah M. Cornell."

Another letter written on yellow stationery, dated November 13, 1832, was unsigned and read:

Miss Cornell—*"I have just received your letter with no small surprise, and will say, I will do all you ask, only keep your secrets. I wish you to write me as soon as you get this, naming some time and place where I shall see you, and then look for answer before I come; and will say whether convenient or not, and will say the time. I will keep your letters till I see you, and wish you to keep mine, and have them with you there at the time. Write soon*—*say nothing to no one. Yours, in haste."*

The letter on pink stationery, also unsigned, and dated November 26, 1832 read:

Dear Sister—*I received your letter in due season and should have answered it before now but I thought I would wait till this opportunity*—*as I told you I am willing to help you and do for you as circumstances are I should rather you would come to this place, Bristol, on the 18th of*

Dec, and stop at the Hotel and stay till six in the evening and then go directly up across the main street to the brick building near to the stone meeting house where I will meet you and talk with you—when you come to the Tavern either enquire for work or go out in the street on pretense of looking for some or something else and I may see you—say nothing about me or my family—should it storm on the 18th come on the 20th if you cannot come and it will be more convenient to meet me at the Methodist meeting house in Somerset just over the ferry on- either of the above evenings I will meet you there at the same time or if you cannot do either I will come to Fall River on one of the above evenings back of the same meeting house where I once saw you—at any hour you say on either of the above evenings when there will be the least passing I should think before the mill stops work—this I will leave with you, if I come, will come, if it does not storm very hard—if it does the first I will come the second write me soon and tell me which—when you write direct your letters to Betsy Hill and not as you have done to me remember this your last letter I am afraid was broken open. Wear your calash not your plain bonnet. You can send your letter by mail . . . let me still enjoin the secret—keep the letters in your bosom or burn them up.

The final letter, also unsigned, written on white stationery and dated December 8, 1832, read: "I will be here on the 20th if pleasant at the place named, at six o'clock. If not pleasant, the next Monday evening. Say nothing, etc."

The deputy post master at the Fall River Post Office where this last letter had been mailed witnessed Avery dropping the letter into a mail slot and took the letter out of the slot noticing it was addressed to S. M. Cornell. There was little doubt in anyone's mind that Avery had written all the letters—the yellow, the pink, and the white—and that each of them was more damning than the next.

The letters, combined with what Dr. Wilbur knew, were enough evidence for the coroner to rule Cornell's death a murder and request that the Fall River and Tiverton authorities issue a warrant for Avery's arrest. What Dr. Wilbur knew about Cornell and Avery was crucial to the case.

Wilbur had met with Cornell in October 1832. According to Wilbur, Cornell told him, "She had come she said to consult him on the subject of her health. She had not been well for some time, and wished to ascertain with certainty the nature of her disease." He asked her to relay her symptoms. Wilbur asked her bluntly if she was married.

"No sir," Cornell told him.

"If you were a married woman, I should be apt to tell you what I thought, but as it is I scarcely know what to say, except it is my opinion you will not be able to work in the factory much longer," he told her. Cornell began to cry.

Wilbur told her, "I only give my opinion, grounded upon the facts you have stated with respect to your ill health, and I may add your too evident distress bespeaks you to have been the prey of a villain; but has not the person who has thus entailed misfortune upon you, the power to take you from the hardships of a factory and place you in a comfortable situation, until you can again resume your employment with safety to yourself?"

"I am afraid he would not be willing to do so," Cornell told him.

"Not be willing?" Wilbur said. "Then he must be a very base man. It certainly is in his place to do so. Who is he?"

Cornell refused to tell him at first but finally, swearing Wilbur to an oath of secrecy, she told him it was Avery who had impregnated her.

"Monstrous," Wilbur said. "And does he preach now?"

Cornell told him that Avery served as a Methodist minister in nearby Bristol, Rhode Island.

Wilbur questioned her regarding where and when her encounter with Avery had taken place. She told him that it took place at a Methodist Camp Meeting in Thompson, Connecticut.

"It was unsought by me for any such purpose, but I trusted myself with him in a lonely place, and he acted a treacherous part," she told him.

Cornell explained that she had been staying in New Hampshire and later went to live with her sister and brother-in-law in Woodstock, Connecticut. She explained that during the summer, she attended a Methodist camp meeting where hundreds of people attended, sleeping overnight in tents during a four-day prayer meeting. She said she was approached by Avery and that they took a walk into the woods far from prying eyes.

According to the account of her sister, "They sat down. . . . At that time, he took hold of her hands, and put one onto her bosom or something like it. She said she tried to get away from him, but could not. She said he then had intercourse with her, and they returned to the camp."

Sarah was advised by her brother-in-law to go to Rhode Island where, if necessary, she could sue Avery for support. Sarah moved to Fall River, Massachusetts, on the Rhode Island border—not far from the town of Bristol where Avery served as a minister and where she knew she could get work in the factories to support herself and her baby.

"Such a man deserves to be exposed. It is a duty you owe not only to yourself but to the public to expose the man. It is outrageous that such a man should continue to deceive the public. I would therefore if I were you boldly go forward and expose him to the world, and compel him by law to do me justice. You would certainly be doing society a service to unmask such a person," Wilbur told her.

"I cannot consent to bring such disgrace and trouble upon the church and upon his innocent family too. He has a worthy woman for a wife, and she and all his innocent children must be disgraced if he is exposed," Cornell said.

That ended their first encounter. There was another some weeks later. Cornell came to Wilbur to ask advice. She explained that she had received a letter from Avery requesting her to come to Bristol and see him there—that he had appointed a time and place, and seemed anxious for the meeting.

The doctor told her that she should compel Avery to reach a financial settlement for support of the unborn child. Cornell said she could not bring herself to do it because Methodist ministers were poor and she doubted very much that Avery had any money to give her.

There was more. Cornell told Dr. Wilbur that Avery had contacted her personally and they had spoken at the Methodist meeting house in Fall River where Avery gave her a medicine that he recommended, in order to abort the child. Wilbur asked to see the medicine and discovered it was oil of tansy, a horrific poison, and that had she taken it, it would have killed her instantly. Wilbur advised her against meeting privately with Avery and begged her not to go to Bristol alone. There was no telling what Avery might do to end this matter. Cornell obviously did not heed Wilbur's cautionary advice.

Wilbur told the coroner about his meetings with Cornell prior to her death and everything he had learned. A warrant for Avery's arrest was issued and a large delegation, with warrant in hand, went to Bristol, Rhode Island, to arrest him and bring him back to Tiverton to stand trial, but Bristol authorities would not release him. They decided that a hearing to determine whether Ephraim Avery would be tried for murder would be held in Bristol. This did not sit well with Fall River and Tiverton authorities.

Avery was neither ignorant of the death of Sarah Cornell nor ignorant of the suspicions leveled against him. He sought counsel from Minister Bidwell and began to accumulate as much evidence as he could regarding Cornell's past indiscretions and bad character. Cornell's reputation preceded her. She had been caught stealing, run out of several Methodist congregations for unbecoming behavior, including running off with a man and later discovered drunk in his arms. Avery too had had his fair share of run-ins with Cornell previously.

Cornell had been born in Vermont in 1802. At twelve years of age, she became an apprentice seamstress. She worked in Norwich, Connecticut, where she was fired from her job for breaking her loom. She moved on to other jobs where she did not fare much better. In Jewett City, Connecticut, she was fired from another seamstress job for promiscuous behavior. Moving to Dorchester, Massachusetts, Cornell joined a Methodist congregation but was forced out because she called the Methodist elders a bunch of old fools. In Slaterville, Rhode Island, she joined another Methodist congregation but was dismissed for lewd behavior.

In 1828, Cornell moved to Lowell, Massachusetts, where she went to work as a weaver in one of the Lowell factories. It was there in Lowell that Cornell first met Avery, who was serving as a minister in the city. Avery had moved to Lowell with his invalid wife, Sophia; his five-year-old son, Edwin; and his infant daughter, Catherine. Cornell became a member of his congregation but soon found herself in trouble again, this time for stealing and for consorting with men and drinking. Avery threatened to have her expelled from the congregation for her behavior, but she promised him she would reform. She offered to do anything for him if he would let her stay as part of the congregation. Avery relented for a time but Cornell's behavior didn't change.

In October 1830, Avery banished Cornell from the Lowell congregation for stealing and lewd behavior. She moved out of Lowell to New Hampshire where she joined another Methodist congregation, this time in Somersworth. When Avery heard of her move, he immediately contacted the minister at the Somersworth congregation warning the minister there of Cornell's questionable behavior. Cornell was once again expelled from the congregation. This time she informed the Somersworth's minister that Avery might have "triumphed over me now. But what care I for Mr. Avery and the Methodist Church? I will have my revenge, though it cost me my life."

Cornell left Somersworth and moved to Woodstock, Connecticut, where she moved in with her sister and brother-in-law. It was while she was there that she attended the camp meeting in Thompson where she claimed she met with Avery and that he took advantage of her. Avery of course denied such behavior. He claimed to have met Cornell at the camp but that his only objective was to inform Cornell that her tarnished reputation would keep her from being part of any Methodist congregation. Cornell's version of the meeting was starkly different. According to Cornell's letter written to her sister, "He did overtake me, outside the fence, and we passed on, arm in arm, into the woods. When in the woods some distance, he asked me to sit down, and I did. I asked him if he had burned my letters, the ones I wrote him from Somersworth, asking to be retained in meeting. No, but there is one condition on which I will settle the difficulty. About this time, he took one of my hands and put one of his own into my bosom. I tried to get away from him, but could not."

Regardless of Avery's desire to accumulate as much evidence as possible regarding Cornell's reputation and behavior, the people of Fall River and Tiverton were intent on prosecuting him on the charge of murder. They felt they had enough evidence to show that Avery had both motive and opportunity to murder Cornell and indeed had done. A contingent of Fall River and Tiverton officials went to Bristol, Rhode Island, to bring Avery back to stand trial. When the group arrived in Bristol, the authorities there informed them that a hearing regarding Avery's guilt or innocence would be held in Bristol, not in Fall River or Tiverton where the murder had taken place. The Fall River contingent relented and returned to Massachusetts empty-handed.

A hearing was held in the courthouse on the Bristol Common. The courtroom was packed. The entire hearing was a fiasco from beginning to end. It began on Christmas Day, December 25, 1832, with Judges John Howe and Levi Haile hearing the case. The prosecution supplied the judges with evidence showing that, despite Avery's claim that he was in Bristol at the time of the murder, he was in fact seen in Tiverton. The court would not allow the various letters into evidence, since it couldn't be proven that they were written by Avery. The court also prohibited testimony from Cornell's sister nor would they allow Dr. Wilbur to testify. Clearly, the deck was stacked against the prosecution. The defense brought in dozens of witnesses that testified to Avery's good character and others who recounted Sarah Cornell's bad reputation. Avery claimed he was out walking on the day Cornell was murdered and although he cited several people who had seen him, none of the so-called witnesses could recall seeing the minister that day.

On January 7, the Bristol court discharged Avery on a legal technicality, noting that the original complaint against Avery had been signed not by the coroner but by the farmer Durfee, on whose land the body had been found. The court also ruled that there was not sufficient evidence to conclude that Avery was guilty on the grounds that the complaint was signed by a private citizen (Durfee) instead of by the coroner, and that there was not much evidence against Avery anyway. That very evening in Fall River, word spread quickly that Avery had been released and that by all accounts the Bristol hearing had been a sham. An angry crowd gathered in the Fall River Congregational Church in Fall River. If the Bristol court would not bring Avery to justice, the angry crowd decided they would.

A new warrant for Avery's arrest was issued by Judge Randall of the Rhode Island Superior Court on the grounds that Avery's hearing was conducted outside the county where the crime had been committed and therefore illegal. Fall River deputy Harvey Hamden headed to Bristol with the new warrant in hand to find and arrest Avery and return him for trial in Newport, Rhode Island, then the country seat. By the time Hamden arrived in Bristol, Avery had fled without a trace and no one would reveal his whereabouts. Avery had correctly assumed that the people of Fall River and Tiverton would not abide by the Bristol ruling and so he fled north to New Hampshire. Hamden somehow managed to pick up Avery's trail, which led him to the town of Rindge, New Hampshire. There he was able to find, confront, and arrest the minister and transport him back to Newport, Rhode Island, to stand trial.

The Rhode Island Supreme Court grand jury indicted Avery for murder in the first degree. His trial opened on May 6, 1833, in the Colony House in Newport. More than 500 spectators crowded into the courtroom and newspaper reporters from as far away as New York City came to cover the sensationally lurid case. Avery was charged with three counts in the indictment, the first for "choking and strangling the deceased"; the second for "tying her to a stake"; and the third for "inflicting various wounds and bruises on the deceased, calculated to cause death." There was no charge issued relating to Cornell's pregnancy.

Avery pleaded not guilty. Albert C. Greene, the state's attorney general, prosecuted the case. Jeremiah Mason of Boston had been hired by Avery's Methodist Congregation to defend him. The trial lasted twenty-seven days. The prosecution called seventy-eight witnesses. Mason called 160, mostly clergymen, to prove that Avery's reputation was impeccable while Cornell's was shocking. Mason's witnesses attacked Cornell's moral standing and her sanity.

Attorney Mason called on an expert in penmanship, a first in forensic science, who testified that the three letters in question—the pink, yellow, and white—were all forged; it was not, the expert concluded to the court, Avery's handwriting. Mason maintained that Cornell had forged the three letters and then hanged herself to incriminate Avery.

Avery's whereabouts on the day Cornell was murdered was called into question and although Mason maintained his client was nowhere near the scene of the murder, claiming he had gone for a long walk on the day in question, Mason could not produce a single witness who could testify that they had seen Avery that day. Conversely, the prosecution was unable to produce any witnesses that saw Avery in Fall River or Tiverton on the day Cornell was killed. It was a moot point for both sides.

Finally, Mason called Dr. Walter Channing, professor of midwifery and medical jurisprudence at Harvard, to the stand. Channing testified that it was impossible to tighten a clove hitch knot, the kind found tied around Cornell's neck, on anyone who resisted, and therefore he concluded Cornell herself tightened the rope when she hung herself. It took the prosecution seven hours to sum up the case to the jury. Mason's summation lasted eight hours. The jury was sent to deliberate on the case on Saturday, June 1. On Sunday, the jury released their verdict: they could not find enough evidence to convict Ephraim Avery of murder. Avery was found not guilty. Avery was discharged—finally a free man.

The Methodist clergy rushed to shake his hand. The majority of the audience, angry about the verdict, filed out of the court loudly proclaiming their disgust and disbelief. Avery returned to his home in Bristol. With the sensational trial concluded, Avery tried to return to his normal life. It would never be. Although the Methodist Bishop appointed him as an assistant minister in the Bristol church, Avery could not face the throngs of people who flocked to his service, many of them angry Fall River and Tiverton citizens who came to glare and taunt him.

He tried preaching in Connecticut but the news of his acquittal had been in all the New England papers and people hissed and booed whenever he tried to speak. He traveled to Boston where a mob of 500 people accosted him threatening to hang him there on the cobblestone streets of Boston. Avery fled for his life. At Durfee's farm, where Cornell's body had been found and where she was now buried, Durfee had constructed a straw effigy of Avery, kneeling in prayer with a rope on his neck. He was burned in effigy twice in Bristol and at least four times in Fall River. There was nowhere Avery could preach and by 1837 he resigned from the Methodist ministry.

In order to escape the constant scrutiny and threats on his life, he moved with his family to Lorain County, Ohio, where he spent the rest of his life working as a farmer. He died in 1869. By then, his infamy was only vaguely recalled. Cornell's body, originally buried on the Durfee farm, was later moved to the Oak Grove Cemetery in Fall River.

Miss Cornell—I will do all you ask, only keep it secret. I wish you to write me as soon as you get this, naming a time and place where I can see you, and wait for my answer before I come . . . I will keep your letter till I see you, and wish you to keep mine, and have them when I see you. Write soon—Say nothing to no one. Yours in haste.

—Ephraim Avery, a letter received
by Maria Cornell, November 13, 1832.

CHAPTER 6

Murder of the Girl in Green

Richard Robinson, 1836

Helen Jewett, a beautiful twenty-three-year-old prostitute, was bludgeoned to death in 1836 in New York City by store clerk Richard Robinson.

Helen Jewett, the beautiful twenty-three-year old prostitute known as "The Girl in Green," in New York City, was turned bloody red when she was bludgeoned to death in 1836 by a jealous suitor who ultimately got away with murder.

AT 3:00 A.M. ON APRIL 10, 1836, HELEN JEWETT'S BODY WAS DISCOVERED lying in her blood-soaked bed by Rosina Townsend. Townsend operated the brothel where Jewett plied her trade. Someone had smashed her skull and set her bed on fire. The murder had taken place sometime after midnight. She was struck on the head three times with a sharp object. The coroner's report later identified it as a hatchet. The coroner concluded that the blows were not expected since there were no signs of struggle. After the lethal blows, the murderer then set fire to Jewett's bed. Townsend discovered the room full of smoke and Jewett's body charred on one side.

The brothel was occupied by nine other women, including Maria Stevens. She occupied the room upstairs opposite Jewett. Around midnight, Stevens was awakened by the sound of a loud thump. She then heard a woman moan. She got out of bed and went to her door and listened. She heard the door open and close across the hall. Next, she heard someone walking down the hall. She assumed Jewett's customer had just left. She opened the door a crack and looked out. There she saw a tall man leave, wearing a cloak and carrying a lamp. She recognized the man as one of Jewett's frequent customers. Sensing nothing out of the ordinary, Stevens returned to bed.

About two hours later, Townsend, the house madam, set out to make her rounds. She always checked the house before retiring for the night. She found a small lamp burning on a table in the hallway downstairs. She was about to pick it up when she noticed that the back door was wide open. It had snowed during the night and the weather was unseasonably cold. She shut the door and locked it. Next, she picked up the lamp in the hallway and headed upstairs to check on the rooms. Once upstairs, Townsend sensed that something was wrong. The door to Jewett's room was ajar. She pushed open the door and saw that billowing black smoke engulfed the room. There were flames lapping along the bed. She rushed away to wake the other women in the house. She threw open a window and called for help, screaming, "Fire!"

A night watchman who had been patrolling the street heard Townsend's cries and rushed into the house. Two other men who had also heard the cries joined him. Several male customers ran out of the place before they could be identified and prevented from leaving. The three watchmen rushed upstairs with Townsend to put out the fire in Jewett's room. It took a few minutes, but they managed to put the fire out before it spread. As the smoke cleared, they saw a woman lay in the once burning bed. They had no doubt she was dead. One arm was raised over her head, the other lay over her chest, and the left side of her body was burned from the fire. Her head had been smashed in and she lay in a pool of blood.

The men asked Townsend if she had seen anyone else in the room that night. She said she had. She told the men she brought champagne to the room earlier that evening and had seen Frank Rivers in the room with Jewett. She remembered he had come in wearing a long dark cloak. The authorities were called. They searched the room and the backyard, where they found a bloodstained hatchet left on the ground and a blood-stained cloak lying in the bushes. It was determined that both belonged to Jewett's killer. The authorities questioned Townsend, Stevens, and the other women in the house. The women testified that Frank Rivers had arrived at the house at 9:00 p.m. He went straight up to Jewett's room on the second floor, and later Townsend was called to deliver a bottle of champagne. Townsend said she saw Rivers lying on Jewett's bed. Stevens testified that she saw the man that had left Jewett's room that evening. She confirmed it was Rivers.

A coroner's inquest was immediately convened at the scene of the crime. The jury at the inquest was made up of men randomly chosen from the crowd gathered in the street outside the house. This was the customary procedure in any case of death from doubtful cause. The jury listened to the testimony of ten witnesses, including Stevens, Townsend, and the other prostitutes. Townsend testified that the man identified as Frank Rivers who had been with Jewett that evening was actually a man named Richard Robinson. He had visited Jewett frequently using the name Frank Rivers. Many young men like Robinson assumed aliases to hide their true identities when consorting with prostitutes. Robinson worked as a clerk in a dry goods store located on Maiden Lane in the city. Based on the testimony of the eye witnesses, especially Stevens, who saw Robinson leaving Jewett's room shortly before the murder, the coroner's jury quickly concluded that "it is the opinion of this Jury from the Evidence before them that the Said Helen Jewett came to her death by a blow or blows inflicted on the head, with a hatchet by the hand of Richard P. Robinson."

Although circumstantial evidence, it was enough to gain an initial indictment against Robinson. Word spread quickly through the city about the gruesome murder. By Sunday afternoon, throngs of curiosity seekers and newspaper reporters crowded around the house where she had been killed. Even the mayor visited the crime scene. The lurid details of the story shocked even New Yorkers and gave birth to sensational journalism. It generated an unprecedented amount of newspaper coverage. People on the streets of New York could talk about nothing else.

The New York City newspapers referred to Jewett as "The Girl in Green." It was the color she preferred to wear that accented her beautiful features. She liked to dress in green and stroll along Broadway, catching the eye of young men she knew or whom she eventually seduced. Beautiful, smart, and sophisticated, at just twenty-three years old, she was one of the most sought-after prostitutes at Townsend's upscale brothel—a four-story brick house located at 41 Thomas Street in lower Manhattan not far from New York's City Hall. It was considered the top-of-the-line brothel where the prostitutes, like Jewett, characteristically earned $3 to $5 per client, a substantial amount in 1836.

Her many clients included lawyers, politicians, wealthy businessmen, and even journalists. Townsend lived on the premises, controlled entree into the establishment, supervised the downstairs socializing parlor, and sold food and liquor to the guests. The girls each paid $10 a week for room and board and maid service for cleaning, laundry, and dressing. Jewett's life was fairly comfortable. She had time to read books and periodicals and to write letters, six or eight per day. She had an expensive wardrobe and jewelry and she never had to cook or clean. She was an independent contractor, choosing her own clients while rejecting others. She was never under the control of Townsend or a pimp.

There was some degree of danger in her lifestyle. Unruly street gangs occasionally descended on the fancy brothels, smashing furniture and mirrors, and, less often, pummeling the inhabitants of the houses, including the prostitutes. Jewett was personally attacked three times in relatively minor incidents. By and large, Jewett was generally safe from violence, largely because she was able to control the conditions of her employment. Most of her customers were regulars with whom she cultivated personal relationships. She carried on an extensive and flirtatious correspondence with many of them and even exchanged presents, books, and tokens of affection like rings and portrait miniatures with a select few.

In 1834, she went to court to lodge a complaint against the man who tripped her. The newspaper reporter covering the court was so captivated by her beauty and charm that he asked her asked her how she came to be a prostitute. The story she told him was a classic seduced and abandoned fantasy; it was printed in the *New York Transcript*. It was here she became known as "The Girl in Green." The story portrayed her as an unfortunate orphan who was sent to boarding school near Boston where a rich merchant's son gained her trust and seduced her. She ended up friendless on the streets of New York where she had to fend for herself, with no other choice than to become a prostitute. The story she had told the reporter, and which was subsequently published, was far from the truth.

Jewett was born Dorcas Doyen in Temple, Maine, into a working-class family. Her father was an alcoholic; her mother died when Jewett was young. From the age of twelve or thirteen, she was employed as a servant girl in the home of Chief Justice Nathan Weston of the Maine Supreme Judicial Court. The judge's family indulged her with more than a basic education and she became a voracious reader. Besides the judge's extensive library, she used a nearby bookstore and lending library that provided her with a constant stream of romantic novels. While there, she was taught how to be and act like a lady of the upper crust. It was her reading that filled her with notions of a life beyond her lowly status as a servant girl.

After five years, she left the judge's home and moved to Portland, Maine, where she worked as a prostitute under an assumed name, which was a typical practice at the time. Three years later, in 1833, she eventually moved to Boston and finally New York City, the capital of commercial sex. At least 2,000 prostitutes worked in the city, most at low rates in the squalid slums. Some, like Jewett, worked out of fashionable brothels that were intertwined into reputable neighborhoods. Women like Townsend usually ran the business. At these upscale brothels, prostitutes made a good and significant income, often earning up to $2,000 a year or more.

No other occupations available to women paid nearly so well. There were no laws at the time that plainly prohibited prostitution, making it illegal. However, authorities could and often did prosecute prostitutes for vagrancy or disorderly conduct. For women in the nineteenth century, prostitution was a last resort, when poverty, dishonor, or abandonment left them with nowhere to go to make a living. But for Helen Jewett, it was a seemingly true calling that she embraced.

One of Jewett's frequent customers was nineteen-year-old Richard P. Robinson. He came from a small town in Connecticut. His father was a large landowner who represented his town in the state legislature. Robinson had lived on his own in New York City since the age of fourteen. His employer, Joseph Hoxie, was active in temperance circles and had helped to found a library for clerks and apprentices to keep them off the streets and into moral reading and lectures. Hoxie did not supervise his clerks very well and Robinson and the young men he associated with often frequented saloons, theaters, and brothels nearly every night.

He lived at a boarding house at 42 Dey Street and shared a room with another young clerk, James Tew. These young men were mostly in their late teens and early twenties. They were not native New Yorkers. They came from towns and villages in New England and upstate New York from the middle- and upper-class homes. Like Robinson, they hoped to be spared from the rural agricultural life of their parents and desired training for a commercial or professional career beyond what their small towns could offer. They came to New York City to learn the business by clerking in various shops and commercial establishments. By day, they penned letters, measured cloth, swept out stores, sold to customers, or perhaps kept the books, learning the cashier's trade. At night, they were on their own, roaming unsupervised and eager to take part in the city's vast social life despite their meager income.

Robinson and Jewett met in June 1835 and within a few weeks became romantically involved. But it was also a stormy relationship. It was reported that he had met Jewett at the theater, where he rescued her from the advances of a drunken ruffian. She gave him her address and he was soon spending a great deal of time with her using the alias of Frank Rivers. He spent an abundant amount of money on her, lavishing her with jewelry and gifts. Although poorly paid, Robinson revealed to her that he was embezzling money from his employer.

He made a dashing figure dressed in his long Spanish cloak. He was handsome and tall, with long curly hair. Jewett appeared to sincerely like Robinson, though he was four years younger, and soon they began exchanging love letters. But as time passed, she found him too indifferent to their future relationship and their letters became more volatile in nature. Although he was involved with Jewett, he was also seeing other women, including the daughter of his employer, Joseph Hoxie. Jewett told Townsend that Robinson intended to break off their relationship so he could marry a respectable girl, most likely Hoxie's daughter. She made vague threats in several of her letters to him to expose him for embezzling from his boss.

He also expressed his misgiving about their relationship. He told her he hated how she made her living and that he could not bear the thought of other men purchasing her. He asked her to give up her life as a prostitute and devote herself solely to him. She refused. He promised to marry her, but she knew he was in no position financially to support her. They fought and broke off their relationship and then reconciled over and over. Finally, he sent her a message vowing he would come to see her but asked her not to tell anyone about his visit. He promised he would be there on Saturday night, April 9, 1836.

Following the coroner's inquest, the authorities arrested Robinson at the boarding house where he was living, 42 Dey Street. They interrogated his roommate, James Tew. When asked to tell what he knew of Robinson's whereabouts on the night in question, Tew told them that he and Robinson had gone for a walk around 7:30 p.m. Tew admitted he was at the brothel on Thomas Street that evening sometime around 9:30 p.m. He said he stayed downstairs and talked to a young woman for only a few minutes. Tew said he went home at 10:30 p.m. and was asleep by 11:15 p.m. He testified Robinson came home later and was in bed when

Tew awoke somewhere around 1:00 a.m. He reportedly asked Robinson what time he had come home. Robinson told him 11:30 p.m.

Instead of going directly to the police station, the authorities took Robinson to the Thomas Street house, letting him know that they believed he had killed a woman there that night.

They led him up the steps and down the hall to Jewett's room. Her body was still lying on the bed and Robinson was forced to look at her. He showed no signs of nervousness or even sorrow. Instead, he claimed he had been home that night, asleep in his bed. Then Robinson made a narcissistic gesture when he told those who were there that under no circumstances would he destroy his bright future by committing such a vicious act of murder. Several police officers led him away to Bridewell, a municipal prison located on Broadway to be held there until the grand jury hearing returned a verdict. Robinson continued to deny his involvement in the murder, but the investigation picked up momentum.

The coverage of Jewett's murder and the subsequent trial of Robinson were decidedly polarizing, with reporters either sympathizing with Jewett and vilifying Robinson or attacking Jewett as a seductress who deserved her fate. *The New York Herald*, edited by James Gordon Bennett, Sr., provided the most comprehensive coverage of the sensational murder. Almost from the beginning and throughout the trial, Bennett insisted that Robinson was the innocent victim of a vicious conspiracy launched by the police and Jewett's madam. He also emphasized the sensational nature of the story and worked to exploit the sexual, violent details of Jewett's death. Eventually, *The New York Herald* would become the most widely read newspaper in the country, due in large part to its shockingly lurid reporting of the Helen Jewett's murder. Comparatively, *The New York Sun* argued on its front pages that Robinson was guilty and that he was able to use money and the influence of wealthy relatives and his employer to buy an acquittal.

On June 2, 1836, less than two months after the murder, Robinson's trial began. It was held on a second-floor courtroom of City Hall. Robinson's family, along with his employer, hired a trio of outstanding lawyers. The lawyers discussed the case with Robinson but soon discovered that he was not quite the gentleman he claimed to be. The authorities found a two-volume diary in his room. In the diary, Robinson disclosed that while he looked innocent and naive, his descriptions of himself in the diaries exposed his treatment of various women, including Jewett, to be shameful and devious. It wasn't long before newspaper reporters began publishing excerpts of the revealing document.

A crowd of over 6,000 people gathered around and inside the building to watch the sensational trial. The authorities guarding the courthouse allowed a few hundred people at a time into the chambers to view the trial and then rotated them out to allow others inside. The overcrowded conditions delayed the proceedings several times. The jury selection from among the twenty-nine citizens who showed up took five hours, and Robinson had to stand for the entire time. He was unemotional and composed as he was charged with one count of willful and deliberate murder.

The prosecution claimed the motive was jealousy. According to the prosecution's claim, Robinson went to Townsend's establishment on the night of Saturday, April 9, 1836, with the intention of murdering Jewett. He brought a hatchet with him. The hatchet was identified as the same type of hatchet sold at the dry goods store where Robinson worked. He confronted Jewett in her room and stated he was going to end their relationship for good because he was intending to marry another woman and demanded that Jewett give back his watch, love letters, and other gifts he had given her, which were in her possession. She refused to give them up. He then took out the hatchet he'd had concealed beneath his cloak and struck her three times on the head. Robinson then lit the bed on fire and then ran from the room and left the house, discarding the hatchet and his cloak outside.

The evidence against Robinson remained largely circumstantial and easily refuted by his defense team. The prosecution was not allowed to enter Robinson's diary into evidence and was only allowed one letter from the volume of incriminating correspondence found in Jewett's possession. Most of the testimony against Robinson came from Townsend and other prostitutes from her brothel; however, in his instructions to the jury, the judge told them that due to the very nature of their unsavory occupation, the prostitutes were not to be believed.

The defense team caught two dubious breaks in the case. The first was when a witness came forward who provided an alibi for Robinson at the time of the murder. Robert Furlong testified that the night the murder took place, Robinson had been in his grocery store smoking, drinking, and engaged in lively conversation. It was conjected that Furlong had been bribed to give his testimony. But given that the prosecution witnesses were prostitutes whose word was suspected anyway, the case against Robinson fell apart.

In the second blow to the prosecution's case, Maria Stevens, the star eyewitness in the case who had seen Robinson leaving Jewett's room the night of the murder, died from an arsenic-laced coffee prior to giving her testimony. Whether it was murder or suicide was never determined. Furlong, the grocery store owner who had come forward with an iron-clad alibi for Robinson, also suspiciously died. Two weeks after the end of the trial, Furlong mysteriously committed suicide by jumping into the Hudson River. Some claimed Furlong, suspected of having been bribed to testify on behalf of Robinson, had demanded further payment of Robinson and his family for giving his testimony and met his untimely death at the hands of paid assassins. None of this, however, could ever be proved.

At the end of the trial, the judge gave his instructions to the jury. He strongly suggested that the prosecution had failed to present its case beyond a reasonable doubt. On the morning of June 8, the jury returned with a verdict of not guilty. They had deliberated for less than a half hour. Robinson began to cry. His family and supporters cheered. Jewett's sympathizers were shocked. The sensational case was over.

Soon afterward, Townsend began to receive death threats. Her customers began to dwindle. Most of her girls left, and within two weeks she was forced to sell some of her furnishings. This resulted in a grisly auction where morbid curiosity seekers paid for pieces from the notorious establishment, especially the murder bed.

Furthering the horror of her murder, Jewett's remains were later exhumed by ghouls and sold to a hospital, where her skeleton was used as a medical exhibit.

To escape his notoriety, Robinson moved to Texas, changed his name, and became a prosperous and respected citizen. He seldom spoke of his murder trial in New York City. He died in 1855, after he contracted a fever. Reportedly, on his deathbed, he repeated the name of Helen Jewett, "The Girl in Green."

Slowly I began to discover the lineaments of the corpse, as one would the beauties of a statue of marble. . . . Not a vein was to be seen. The body looked as white—as full—as polished as the pure Parian marble. The perfect figure—the exquisite limbs—the fine face—the full arms—the beautiful bust—all—all surpassing in every respect the Venus de Medicis.
— JAMES GORDON BENNETT, *THE NEW YORK HERALD*, APRIL 12, 1836

The excitement and surprise which had been 'exhibited at the City Hall during the closing, scenes of the trial, extended itself the next morning throughout the entire community, and before night a weight of condemnation had accumulated against the prosecuting powers, that not only appalled those of them against whom it was directed, but struck a new terror into the bosom of Robinson himself. Passionate execrations could be heard along the street against the monster who had escaped. It was the admission at every bar-room that the accused was guilty of the crime alleged against him; and even the papers, usually so servile to the expressed opinion of twelve numbskulls or twelve knaves, declared there could be no doubt of his guilt.
— GEORGE WILKES, *THE LIVES OF HELEN JEWETT AND RICHARD P. ROBINSON*, 1849

CHAPTER 7

Dead Man Strolling

John Webster, 1849

Harvard professor John Webster was executed for killing the prominent Boston businessman George Parkman.

*In 1849, wealthy Boston businessman and physician George Parkman
went missing for nearly a week before police found his body, or at least
parts of it.*

ON FRIDAY, NOVEMBER 23, 1849, GEORGE PARKMAN SET OUT ON HIS
daily rounds through Boston and Cambridge, Massachusetts, to collect
the debts on his many accounts. As usual, his lanky stooped figure, chin
out, marched briskly on his routine rounds through the city. He owned
many tenement buildings that he personally collected rents from, and
although he generously lent money to those in need, he also kept strict
track of all his accounts.

He made his way religiously along the street, stopping at various ten-
ements and stores to collect his rents. People said they could set their
watches by his daily routine. Many also wondered how he could carry so
much money around with him during his daily debt collection without
fearing robbery or worse. Regardless, Parkman always kept to his assigned
task. According to one report, "One woman who owed him money fled
from him when he demanded the dollar he had seen in her hand as she
tried to pay for food." He expected people to live up to their agreements,
and he told them so in a sharp voice. At times, he even got aggressive
about it.

Although he was generous lending money to those in financial need,
he expected to be paid back promptly. Parkman made his fortune from
rents and from what he loaned. He was adamant about making people
pay what they owed. He stopped at several stores and at one store, he
bought a head of lettuce and stated that he would come back for it later
rather than have to carry it with him as he made his rounds. Although
earnest about his daily collections, he was also fastidious about dinner
with his wife and hadn't missed his regular 2:00 p.m. dinner with her in all
their thirty-three years of marriage. But this day was different. He didn't
return home for dinner that day. He never even returned to the store
where he had left the head of lettuce he had purchased. He was reportedly last seen at 1:30 p.m. that day in Cambridge at the Harvard Medical
College. When he didn't come home, his wife contacted the police, who
began an investigation immediately.

"Old Chin" was a well-known figure on the streets of Boston because of his daily jaunts throughout the city. Always dressed in a stovepipe top hat and somber frockcoat, Parkman was tall and thin, with a large jutting chin, that gave him the nickname "Old Chin" among those who knew and saw him on his daily treks. He was never called this to his face. A frugal man, he didn't own a horse and abstained from taking carriages. Oliver Wendell Holmes, Sr. said of him that "he abstained while others indulged, he walked while others rode, he worked while others slept."

Fifty-nine-year-old George Parkman was a highly respected and accomplished member of the city's wealthiest families. By the 1840s, Boston was the epicenter to many of the country's wealthiest families who held distinguished positions within American society, education, business, and politics. They were often referred to as "blue bloods," or Boston Brahmin—members of the city's traditional wealthy upper class. They were active in charitable and social causes, including support-ing educational institutions such as the Harvard University in nearby Cambridge.

Parkman was an esteemed physician, businessman, and philanthro-pist. His inherited wealth came from owning large swaths of income properties in Boston's West End, abutting the Charles River, and proper-ties in Ohio and Maine. He was reported to have been worth approxi-mately $5 million by today's monetary standards. As a child, he had been in poor health. Subsequently, he studied medicine at Harvard, where he became interested and active in the treatment and care of the mentally ill. He donated his time and energy raising money for the establishment of a mental hospital connected to Massachusetts General Hospital in Boston and the McLean Asylum for the Insane.

The last confirmed sighting of Parkman was at 1:45 p.m. when he was seen entering the Harvard Medical College building on North Grove Street at 1:45 p.m. where he had gone to meet with Harvard chemistry professor John Webster. Webster had borrowed a considerable amount of money from Parkman and had reneged on paying it back. At Harvard, Parkman met with the Harvard cashier and asked him to provide him with the money from the sale of tickets to Webster's lecture as partial payment for the debt he owed him. Earlier that same day, Webster had gone to Parkman's Walnut Street home and arranged to meet him at the medical college that afternoon.

The leading theory proposed by the authorities was that Parkman had been robbed and murdered by Irish immigrants, who had been flooding into Boston since the potato famine devastated Ireland in the mid-1840s. There were others who opined that Parkman just left the city of his own accord. He was known to be eccentric and his eccentricities knew no bounds. Abruptly leaving without telling anyone of his whereabouts would not be beyond his nature, or so they believed. His wife knew otherwise.

Other rumors soon circulated that he'd been held up, his money stolen, and his body thrown into the Charles River. The Boston police searched the river and harbor and turned up nothing. They also searched neighboring towns to see if Parkman had been sighted in any of the vicinities, but again they found nothing. Search parties made up of police and concerned citizens and family were formed and searched day and night, but they too turned up with no sign of him. Several thousand broadsides were distributed seeking information on "Old Chin's" disappearance, but no one reported having seen him.

Since Webster was reportedly the last man to have seen Parkman at the Harvard Medical School the day of his disappearance, he was one of the first persons questioned. Because Parkman was reportedly last seen at the medical school, the police searched the place twice, checking classrooms, lecture halls, and various laboratories and vaults, but they found nothing to indicate that Parkman had even been there. They also searched many of the nearby buildings, apartments, and homes owned by Parkman in Cambridge.

Webster was a professor of chemistry and mineralogy at Harvard and had earned his medical degree from the university. He was reported to have financial problems and had been forced to give up a mansion he had built in Cambridge because he was in debt to a number of friends and colleagues. His salary at the college and earnings from his lectures could not cover his expenses. Webster had high social aspirations for himself and his family that he could not financially afford. He deceived his family by borrowing money to pay for their home and upkeep, putting up household belongings as well his valuable cabinet of mineral specimens as collateral.

Webster first borrowed $400 from Parkman in 1842, and in 1847, he gave Parkman a note for approximately $2,400, which represented the unpaid balance. In 1848, he borrowed $1,200 from another person, using property that he had already used for his loan from Parkman as collateral. When Parkman learned of it, he was outraged and decided to confront Webster. Questioned by the police, Webster told them he had been to Parkman's home the morning of the disappearance to arrange to pay off a portion of his debt. Parkman, he said, came to the college, and stated he had paid Parkman a sum of $483.64 to pay off part of his debt. He said Parkman was satisfied with the payment and had promised that he would go right away to have the payment recorded by the city clerk to clear the debt. Parkman left without further incident and that was the last time he saw him.

Webster told the police he was worried that someone had robbed Parkman and the debt was not cleared. Further, he told the police that he worked a little longer at the college that day and went home at 6:00 p.m. and attended a party at the house of friends later that evening. The friends confirmed that Webster had attended their party. The police appeared satisfied with Webster's explanation.

On Sunday, November 25, Webster went to visit Parkman's wife and family. He explained to them the same thing he had told to the police, but there was something amiss about it all. He told them that he had read about the disappearance in the papers and thought that he should come and explain what he knew. After his explanation, according to reports, "he got to his feet, gave a stiff bow, and left. He failed to inquire how the family was doing or to offer the merest civility. It was an odd manner, and one that the grieving family would have cause to remember later that week."

Webster's appointment at Harvard was due to Parkman's recommendation and yet his explanation to his wife was cold and mechanical. He didn't appear concerned about the ongoing investigation. In light of Webster's explanation, there were some who wondered where Webster had come up with the money to pay Parkman back. On more than one occasion, Parkman had commented on Webster's dire financial situation noting that Webster had borrowed from several people and had been unable to keep up interest payments on any of those loans. Something just didn't seem right.

On November 26, a $3,000 reward was offered and the family had 28,000 copies of a poster printed and distributed. The police investigation into Parkman's disappearance remained stymied. Although Webster's explanation had been accepted by the authorities, there was one person who wasn't buying it—Ephraim Littlefield, the college janitor. Five days after Parkman's disappearance, Littlefield began his own investigation.

The new Harvard Medical College was built in 1846 and Ephraim Littlefield had been the janitor there since 1842. He and his wife lived in the basement of the college, next door to Webster's laboratory. He knew Webster and many of the other Harvard professors and doctors and often observed their study of medicine, including the dissection of cadavers for the study of human anatomy. He cleaned and maintained the doctors' rooms and laboratories. To supplement his meager income, Littlefield obtained cadavers for dissection at a price of about $25 a body, selling them to students and professors.

He became suspicious when, on the day of Parkman's visit to Webster, he discovered that the laboratory door was bolted shut and the wall by the furnace red-hot. Littlefield told the police he had run into Webster on the street later in the week and said Webster questioned him whether he had seen Parkman at the school the week before. Littlefield admitted that he had at around 1:30 on that Friday afternoon. According to Littlefield, Webster struck his cane on the ground and continued to ask him a series of questions: Had Littlefield seen Parkman anywhere in the building? Had he seen him after 1:30 p.m.? Had Parkman been in Webster's own lecture room? Littlefield shook his head to these queries.

Webster then repeated the details of his meeting with Parkman in the same manner that he'd recited them to Parkman's family. He was very precise about the amount he owed Parkman and the fact that the debt had been cleared. Webster said more in this single encounter than he'd said to Littlefield in their entire time together at the college. Littlefield found the whole exchange disturbing.

On November 27, two days after Parkman had disappeared, Webster came into his office early and Littlefield watched under a door as Webster moved from the furnace to the fuel closet and back. Littlefield observed Webster make eight separate trips, and later in the day, his furnace was burning so hard that the wall on the other side was hot to the touch. When Webster was gone, Littlefield let himself into the room through a window. All the doors had been locked by Webster. Once inside, Littlefield made a strange discovery. The kindling barrels were nearly empty, though they had only been recently filled, and there were wet spots in places where there shouldn't have been. He placed his finger into the wet spot and briefly tasted it. It smelled and tasted like acid.

This made Littlefield more suspicious. He took it upon himself to break into Webster's laboratory by patiently chiseling his way through one of the lab's brick walls. While the police and press were looking for leads in the case, Littlefield was going underground—literally—in search of Parkman. Once inside Webster's laboratory, he made a horrific discovery. To his horror, he found the partial remains of a human body, including portions of the legs and pelvis of a man hidden inside the laboratory. Littlefield quickly informed the police who searched Webster's laboratory and found more remains, charred and half-destroyed, inside the furnace. The police surmised the remains belonged to Parkman and immediately arrested Webster and charged him with Parkman's murder. A distraught Webster claimed his innocence.

When the story broke, the city was horrified and fascinated. The press reported every gory detail. The motive appeared to be money. The police, press, and public opinion all came to the same conclusion: Webster had killed Parkman out of a desire to be free of his humiliating debt. Webster attempted to blame Littlefield for the murder. When he was informed that the authorities had searched his laboratory and found only parts of the body, Webster claimed that Littlefield was the only other person besides himself with access to the laboratory and that it was Littlefield who had killed Parkman and dismembered his body in the laboratory. When the police refused to accept his story, Webster put something into his mouth, which he later admitted was poison. The pill he took only made him ill.

The police soon determined that Webster had killed Parkman, dismembered him, and burned the remains in the laboratory furnace. Littlefield had found a bone fragment in the laboratory furnace and showed it to the police. A coroner's jury was assembled to make a judgment about the disposition of the case. Before they began deliberation, the coroner and the police examined a sink that appeared to be recently gouged in numerous places, strange acid stains on the floor and steps, and the contents of the furnace, from which they removed some coins, a few buttons, and more bone fragments, including a jaw bone with teeth. Then they opened a chest where they discovered an armless, headless torso. Investigators determined that the head had been sawed off and located a blood-stained saw nearby. Next, they found a thigh stuffed inside the torso, with the heart and other organs missing. Parkman's wife was called in and, although shaken to her core, she identified the ghastly remains as her husband. Parkman's brother-in-law also identified the body.

Continued searches turned up bloody clothing belonging to Webster. Testing on the various stains found in Webster's laboratory were identified as copper nitrate, a substance effective for removing blood. Dr. Jeffries Wyman arrived to identify the bone fragments. Since they were already at a medical college with good facilities for the examination of a body, they laid out the parts, tested them, and wrote up thorough descriptions. They speculated that a hole found underneath the left breast might have been the stab that had killed Parkman. Parkman was laid to rest on December 6, 1849, and thousands lined the streets for the funeral. Some 5,000 people even toured the crime scene.

On January 26, 1850, the grand jury indicted Webster for the murder. Despite the charges against Webster, the Boston Brahmins were reluctant to believe that one of their own had done the horrific deed. Webster chose two attorneys to defend him. They were Harvard graduates Edward Dexter Sohier and Pliny T. Merrick. Sohier had previously handled Webster's financial matters but was inexperienced in criminal law. Merrick was more experienced in criminal law.

Webster refused to discuss a defense strategy with them and instead gave them his written statements about the case professing his innocence.

Neither lawyer presented Webster's claim that Littlefield lied and was probably the real killer.

The trial began on March 19, 1850, with Chief Justice Lemuel Shaw of the Massachusetts Supreme Judicial Court presiding. Shaw was a Harvard Law School graduate.

Associate Justices Samuel Wilde, Charles A. Dewey, and Theron Metcalf were also present. The trial took twelve days. More than 60,000 people witnessed at least part of the trial. Tickets to the trial were handed out to the crowds waiting outside the courtroom. Journalists from as far away as London, Paris, and Berlin covered the proceedings.

Leading the prosecution were Massachusetts attorney general John Clifford, who limited his role to opening and closing statements, and George Bemis, another Harvard Law School graduate. Bemis was a noted legal scholar and respected, demanding prosecutor. On the first day of the trial, Clifford gave a three-hour opening statement presenting the facts and evidence in the case. Bemis then began his examination of witnesses.

Oliver Wendell Holmes, Sr., the dean of Harvard Medical College, a position that had been endowed by Parkman, testified that it was his belief that the body had been dismembered by someone with a knowledge of dissection and anatomy, and that the corpse's build was "not dissimilar" to that of George Parkman.

Dr. Nathan Keep, Parkman's dentist, swore that the jawbone found in Webster's laboratory belonged to Parkman. He testified that he could identify the false teeth found in the furnace, recognizing them from work he had done on the victim. Littlefield took the stand and testified all the details he had previously conveyed to the police. Littlefield's wife also testified for the prosecution. The prosecution told the jury about Webster's debts and financial problems and about the money he owed Parkman. Webster's defense attorneys spent two days attempting to refute the prosecution's case. Sohier gave a long speech complaining that Webster could not defend himself. At the time, Massachusetts's law did not let capital murder defendants, like Webster, address the court and could only make one unsworn speech to the jury at the end of the trial.

Sohier asserted that the prosecution had failed to show beyond a reasonable doubt that Webster was the killer or even how Parkman had died. He called twenty-three character witnesses and seven others who claimed to have seen Parkman after his supposed time of disappearance. Sohier called medical experts, some of whom had testified for the prosecution, who agreed that it was difficult to identify the body or how the man had died. He disputed Parkman's dentist. He called the prosecution's case purely circumstantial at best. Webster's defense team gave a six-hour closing speech. They argued that even if the remains that were found in the laboratory were definitely Parkman's, which they disputed, anyone could have killed him and disposed of his body. Webster himself then took the stand, against his attorneys' strong advice and in a fifteen-minute speech he criticized his attorneys and presented his own version of the evidence.

Judge Shaw then made a historic statement to the jury, one that had a lasting impact on the legal system. He told the jury that they only needed to find beyond a reasonable doubt that the *corpus delicti* (the body) was Parkman's. At the time, the legal standard in murder cases was proof "to an absolute certainty" that the dead body was that of the victim. In a murder case, this had always meant that prosecutors must physically produce the corpse of the person allegedly murdered. Shaw made it possible for the jury to conclude from the overwhelming circumstantial and medical evidence presented that Webster had murdered Parkman. The jury began deliberations with a prayer and then reviewed the evidence. It took less than three hours of deliberation for the jury to find Webster guilty.

On April 1, 1850, Judge Shaw directed "that you, John W. Webster, be removed from this place, and detained in close custody in the prison of this county; and thence taken . . . to the place of execution, and there be hung by the neck until you are dead. And may God, of His infinite goodness, have mercy on your soul!"

Reactions throughout the city were sharply divided. The *Evening Bulletin* wrote, "Scarcely one man in ten thousand can be found who does not agree with us in the opinion that the evidence for the defense was sufficient to create a doubt of the unhappy man's guilt." Another Boston newspaper, *The Massachusetts Ploughman*, wrote, "We have scarcely met a man of intelligence, since the evidence has all come out, who did not profess to believe in Webster's guilt."

Webster's lawyers submitted a petition for a writ of error against Judge Shaw and his instructions to the jury. The hearing was held before Shaw and his four associates on June 12.

The writ was denied. Webster appealed to Governor George N. Briggs for a pardon, asserting his innocence. In June, while being held in Boston's Leverett Street Jail, awaiting execution, Webster broke down and wrote a full confession. He admitted to killing Parkman in self-defense when he had become aggressive over the debt. He said that it was an unpremeditated rage, an act of passion and provocation, and not a malicious murder. He said that Parkman "was speaking and gesticulating in the most violent and menacing manner." Webster claimed that in his fury he "seized whatever thing was handiest; it was a stick of wood, and dealt him an instantaneous blow with all the force that passion could give it. It was on the side of his head, and there was nothing to break the force of the blow. He fell instantly upon the pavement. There was no second blow. He did not move."

Had Webster made the confession at trial and believed by the jury, he could have received a lighter sentence based on a plea of temporary insanity. But it was too late for him to escape the hangman. His confession did not persuade the governor to commute his sentence. Despite many calls for a commutation, the governor remained unmoved. The sentence was final. Engraved invitations to the execution were sent out by various wealthy families connected to the Parkmans.

On August 30, 1850, John Webster was taken to the gallows and hanged. He died within four minutes and was later interred at Copp's Hill Burying Ground. His body was disguised to prevent body snatchers from stealing it. His execution put an end to one of the most sensational scandals to rock Boston society.

The case had an enduring impact on the American legal and medical systems. It was the first time dental evidence and scientific testimony were accepted in a murder trial. It was one of the first cases to use forensic evidence to identify a body. The case also made medical experts central figures in the evaluation of murder investigations. After the hanging, Parkman's widow was the first contributor to a fund created for Webster's impoverished widow and children. The sensational publicity surrounding the case was intensely distressing to Parkman's widow and children. They became recluses in their home at 33 Beacon Street, and neither of Parkman's two children, Harriet and George, ever married. When their mother died in 1877, they inherited the entire Parkman estate. After his sister's death in 1885, George Jr. was the sole heir to their significant fortune. At the time of his death in September 1908, the estate was valued at nearly $5.5 million. The estate was bequeathed to the City of Boston, one of the largest bequests ever made to it.

> *I saw nothing but the alternative of a successful removal and conceal-ment of the body, on the one hand, and of infamy and destruction on the other. The first thing I did, as soon as I could do anything, was to drag the body into the private room adjoining. There I took off the clothes, and began putting them into the fire which was burning in the upper laboratory—They were all consumed there that afternoon, with papers, pocket book, or whatever else they may have contained. I did not examine the pockets, nor remove anything except the watch. I saw that, or the chain of it, hanging out, and I took it and threw it over the bridge as I went to Cambridge. My next move was to get the body into the sink which stands in the small private room. By set-ting the body partially erect against the corner, and getting up into the sink myself, I succeeded in drawing it up. There it was' entirely dismembered. It was quickly done, as a work of terrible and desperate necessity. The only instrument used was the knife found by the officers in the tea-chest, and which I kept for cutting corks. . . . While dismem-bering the body a stream of was running through the sink, carrying off the blood in a pipe that passed down through the lower laboratory. There must have been a leak in the pipe, for the ceiling below was stained immediately round it. There was a fire burning in the furnace of the lower laboratory. Littlefield was mistaken in thinking there had never been a fire there. He had probably never kindled one, but I had done it myself several times. . . . The head and viscera were put into that furnace that day, and the fuel heaped on.*
>
> —JOHN WEBSTER, "THE EXTRAORDINARY CONFESSION
> OF DR. JOHN WHITE WEBSTER," 1850.

CHAPTER 8

The Abortion Murder

Dr. James Harvey Smith, 1850

In Saco, Maine, in 1850, a young, unmarried textile mill worker, Mary Bean, sought an abortion to hide her shameful pregnancy but died from complications.

In Saco, Maine, in 1850, a young, unmarried, textile mill worker, Mary Bean, sought an abortion to hide her shameful pregnancy but died from complications, and her killer sought to hide the botched operation in a gruesome fashion.

ON APRIL 13, 1850, IN SACO, MAINE, OSGOOD STEVENS, A FOURTEEN-year-old boy, was helping a neighbor clear a brook when he happened on a large plank of wood that was stuck in a culvert, damming the flow of the water. Stevens was a strong young man but the plank was heavier than he anticipated. Using both hands and all his strength he managed to drag the plank out of the culvert, flipping it over as he did and what he found tied to it caused him to convulse in terror. On the underside of the plank was the decomposing body of a young woman. She was scantily dressed in a sheer bed slip and dark blue stockings and her face was covered with a faded calico apron. When Stevens untied the apron, he saw that the woman's face was all but eaten away by animals.

Word spread quickly through the small town. Soon a crowd gathered along the banks of the brook where the body still tied to the plank had been laid out on the shore. Both the sheriff and the coroner were called. The body was taken to the coroner's office where an autopsy concluded that the young woman had died from complications from an abortion. At the time, abortion was considered a crime, although infrequently prosecuted. In 1841, passage of a Maine law had made abortion illegal, yet at the same time, over-the-counter medicines to induce abortion were openly sold. Regardless of the social or legal ramification of abortions, the fact that the young woman had died as the result of one was considered murder.

The identity of the young woman remained a mystery for several days. She had been given the alias, Mary Bean, by Dr. James Harvey Smith, the local physician. She had been living in Smith's home prior to her death. Her real name was Berengera Caswell. She was originally from Brompton, Quebec, and had traveled to New England with her two sisters, Ruth and Thais, to find work in the textile mills. She had taken a circumspect route ending up in Saco. Single young women in their late teens to early twenties made up the largest portion of the textile industry workforce throughout New England in the mid-1800s. The rapid development of the mills created a great number of opportunities for young women throughout the rural region. In the past, young women like Caswell lived at home waiting to be married and were engaged primarily in household duties or in spinning yarn or making household products like candles or weaving. The textile mills opened exciting new opportunities for financial independence as well as a chance to move out from under the yoke of their parents. Along with these new opportunities came a vast number of social dangers and temptations. The attitude of the time is clear in an 1842 pamphlet, *Mary Bean: The Factory Girl. A Domestic Story, Illustrative of the Trials and Temptations of Factory Life, Founded on Recent Events*, which claims, "Not unfrequently impatient of restraint, and indisposed to listen to the voice of counsel, the unthinking female is ensnared in the toils of the destroyer, and being insidiously led onward, step by step, she awakes from her dream of fancied happiness, but to mourn over her dishonor, and the destruction of her cherished hopes."

Although parents worried about their young daughters moving off on their own to new cities and towns to work, many believed that their children would remain safe on their own and so far from home, since the living arrangement was in a company-owned boarding houses under the watchful eye of older matrons who would oversee their comings and goings. Accordingly, "strict rules and curfews would keep these daughters of New England safe from harm."

Caswell and her two sisters first settled in the factory town of Lowell, Massachusetts. Ruth married and remained in Lowell, while Berengera and Thais moved to Manchester, New Hampshire, to work at the Amoskeag Mill. There, she worked putting in twelve-hour days and earning approximately $3.25 per week. In the summer of 1849, the twenty-one-year-old girl met William Long, who worked in the machine shop at the Amoskeag Mill, and began their romance.

Their relationship lasted through the summer of 1849 when Long was fired from his job at the mill and returned to his hometown of Biddeford, Maine. Caswell left Manchester and moved to Salem, Massachusetts. In November, she realized she was pregnant and went looking for Long in Biddeford, hoping he would do the honorable thing by her.

If they married, the stigma of "unwed motherhood would be removed." If not, she would be forever chastened as a fallen woman with a bastard child. When she confronted Long, he told her he did not want to marry her. Instead, he pursued the advice of a friend and confidant, his Biddeford mill manager, who suggested a possible solution: abortion. Abortion was a legal procedure in 1849, although not a topic that was openly discussed.

Long convinced her to go to Dr. James Smith, a Saco, Maine, physician, who had a practice out of his Storer Street home. He was known to carry out such operations. She met with Smith, and it was Smith who gave her the alias of Mary Bean to keep her identity secret from a prying public.

He treated her first with herbal medicines that then were used frequently by physicians to induce a miscarriage. When this didn't work, he undertook a risky surgical procedure. Although the operation ended her pregnancy, an infection took hold and with no known antibiotics to fight it, she died less than a week later.

Although Caswell's face was unrecognizable and since there was no DNA testing, fingerprints, or dental records to use, several people in Saco managed to identify her. Along with her identity, investigators discovered that the white-washed plank her body had been tied to came from the floor in Smith's stable. Smith admitted that Bean had been staying with him and that he had been treating her for typhoid. Smith was a "botanical doctor," reportedly only using herbal remedies and was not, according to records, university-trained or in any way accredited. He was born in Vermont and had traveled around New England before settling in Saco because of the growth of the textile mills and the town's population. The more people, the more illnesses that needed treating. Although unconfirmed, it was long rumored that Smith was not his real name and that he had a shady past. Among other things, Smith was a known abortionist.

Smith was ultimately accused of killing Mary Bean while performing an abortion. He denied it and claimed she had died of typhoid. Her body was examined for signs of typhoid. None was found. Caswell's lover was located. He admitted that he had contacted Smith the previous autumn about terminating the girl's pregnancy. The woman, however, was not named Mary Bean. Long testified that he asked Smith if he wanted to know the name of the girl and Smith reportedly declined. He called her "Mary Bean," he said, because "Bean" was a code word he and his associates used previously to hide nefarious activity.

It was revealed that Caswell had moved into Dr. Smith's house while he treated her. Smith first tried giving her extracts from a juniper bush to stimulate uterine contraction and end the pregnancy. When this didn't work, she agreed to a more drastic approach. According to testimony, Smith used an eight-inch wire instrument with a hook on the end to scrape loose the fetus. Although the abortion was successful, during the procedure, Smith accidentally punctured her uterus leaving a gash. The wound quickly became infected and the infection spread through her body. She remained at Smith's house for a week suffering from the infection and died on December 22. Smith needed to get rid of the body to avoid drawing attention to his abortion practice. He tied her body to a plank from his stable and placed it in Woodbury Brook which ran near his house. From there he expected it to float down to the Saco River and ultimately into the ocean. He did not know that the body had only traveled a few yards before getting stuck in the culvert.

In April 1850, a coroner's inquest was held. It aroused great and wide public interest and sensational press coverage. The largest meeting room in Saco had to be used to accommodate more than 600 spectators. Several doctors testified to Caswell's condition in explicit detail, using language too graphic for the newspapers. Several of Smith's neighbors testified to his ongoing abortion practice and William Long testified about taking Caswell to Dr. Smith's house for her abortion. The star witness was Ann Covney, a twelve-year-old Irish immigrant, who was working as a hired girl in Smith's house at the time of Caswell's death. She testified to seeing Smith use abortion tools on Caswell and other girls, and she was an eyewitness to Caswell's death. Smith was ultimately charged with murder.

Smith hired Nathan Clifford, a former US attorney general who was later appointed to the US Supreme Court in 1858. The trial began in January 1851 and was a replay of the coroner's inquest, with the same witnesses giving the same testimony. Clifford tried to place the blame on William Long as Caswell's seducer. According to the newspaper

The Maine Democrat, "[the] argument was ingenious and forcibly presented but he labored under the embarrassment of having the law and evidence against him."

The jury deliberated just two hours before handing down a verdict of guilty of murder in the second degree. Smith was sentenced to life in prison. His attorney appealed the verdict, claiming Smith was not guilty of murder but of performing a botched abortion. Maine's abortion law had two possible punishments, state prison or a fine plus time in county jail. Accordingly, he also argued that the abortion law punished those with intent to destroy an unborn child, but the indictment charged Smith with "intent to cause and procure the said Berengera to miscarry and bring forth the said child." In legal jargon, a miscarriage could bring forth a live, viable child. In April 1852, the Maine Supreme Court overturned the murder verdict and, since Smith had already served enough time for a manslaughter sentence, he was set free. Smith died three years later of tuberculosis, which he contracted in prison.

By 1850, tales of factory girls seduced and ruined had become cliché. The story of Mary Bean's murder was written about in two short books: *Mary Bean, the Factory Girl; or The Victim of Seduction,* published in 1850; and *A Full and Complete Confession of the Horrid Transactions in the Life of George Hamilton: The Murderer of Mary Bean, the Factory Girl,* published in 1852. In both books, Long was renamed George Hamilton and was portrayed as an evil seducer who was much more a vile cad than his real-world counterpart. They were both cautionary tales; the first warns young women to shun temptation by saying home, close to hearth and family; the second warns young men of the dangers of evil companions.

Thais Caswell planned to take her sister's body back to Quebec but was unable to. She remains buried in Manchester, New Hampshire. Her name was added to the family monument in Greenlay Protestant Cemetery in Quebec.

Although abortion was a legal procedure in 1849, Caswell's subsequent death was considered a crime. With public suspicion already aroused by Smith's practice, the doctor attempted to conceal Caswell's death by tying her to a board and placing her in a brook that fed into the Saco River. His plan was foiled when the board became wedged as the brook passed underneath Storer Street on April 1850, Caswell's body was discovered and Smith was charged with murder. Hundreds of residents from across southern Maine followed the sensational case and waited outside the courthouse for the latest information.

—"THE MURDER OF MARY BEAN,"
MAINE HISTORY ONLINE

CHAPTER 9

Prince of Poisoners

William Palmer, 1856

London physician William Palmer poisoned at least sixteen people including several of his own children in 1856.

Although London physician William Palmer had sworn the Hippocratic Oath to heal the sick and infirmed, greed and gambling debts led him to poison at least sixteen people including several of his own children in 1856.

DR. WILLIAM PALMER'S LIFE WAS SPIRALING OUT OF CONTROL. HE OWED incredible amounts on gambling debts especially to a friend, John Cook, and had no way of paying them off. Palmer decided there was only one way out—he decided to poison Cook with strychnine in order to hide the debts he owed him.

Cook was a sickly young man with an inherited fortune. In London, in November 1855, Palmer and Cook went to the horse races and bet on various horses. Cook won while Palmer lost a substantial sum of money. Cook and Palmer had a celebration party at a local drinking establishment but Cook complained that his drink burnt his throat. Palmer responded by making a scene in attempting to convince onlookers that there was nothing wrong with Cook's drink. Afterward, Cook became violently sick and told two friends that he believed that Palmer was poisoning him.

Having recovered from his illness, Cook met with Palmer for coffee and soon found himself sick once again. At this point, Palmer assumed responsibility for Cook, taking him into his home to care for him. Cook's lawyer sent over a bowl of soup that Palmer had in his possession before he sent it to the kitchen to be reheated. A chambermaid took two spoonsful of the soup and subsequently fell ill. Cook was given the rest of the soup, and his condition became worse. Palmer had purchased three grains of strychnine and put the grains into two pills, which he then administered to Cook. Not long after Palmer administered the poison, Cook died. He was not Palmer's only victim. Nearly a dozen people died at the hands of the villainess and unrepentant Palmer; however, he was only convicted for the 1855 murder of his friend Cook.

In one of the most sensational cases of the nineteenth century, Palmer was dubbed the "Prince of Poisoners" by the London newspapers, which covered the story in breathless detail. Newspapers printed every rumor and accusation that reporters could extract from local gossips and, if the reports were to be believed, Palmer was guilty of poisoning at least sixteen people, including his mother-in-law; four of his five children, who died of convulsions before their first birthdays; his wife; and his drunken brother. Palmer made large sums of money from the deaths of his wife and brother after collecting on their life insurance policies and by defrauding his wealthy mother out of thousands of dollars, all of which he lost at the horse races. Palmer was an incorrigible gambler and his motive was money.

As a seventeen-year-old, Palmer worked as an apprentice at a Liverpool chemist but was fired after three months following allegations that he stole money. He then studied medicine in London and qualified as a physician in August 1846. After returning to Staffordshire later that year, he met plumber and glazier George Abley at the Lamb and Flag public house in Little Haywood and challenged him to a drinking contest. Abley accepted, and an hour later was carried home, where he died in bed later that evening. Nothing was ever proven, but locals noted that Palmer had an interest in Abley's attractive wife.

Palmer returned to his home town of Rugeley to open his practice, and in 1847, he married Ann Thornton. His new mother-in-law had inherited a small fortune but she died under mysterious circumstances in January 1849, two weeks after coming to stay with Palmer. Palmer was disappointed with the inheritance he and his wife received from her death, expecting it to have been much more. He became interested in horse racing and borrowed money from Leonard Bladen, a man he met at the races. Bladen then died under mysterious circumstances at Palmer's house in May 1850. His wife was surprised to find that her husband died with little money on him, despite having recently won a large sum at the races; his betting books were also missing, so there was no evidence of his having lent Palmer any money.

His first son, William Brookes Palmer, was born in 1850 and was the only child to outlive his father. The Palmers had four more children who all died in infancy, the cause of death listed as convulsions. Since infant mortality was not uncommon at the time, these deaths were not initially viewed as suspicious, although after Palmer's conviction in 1856 there was speculation that he had administered poison to the children to avoid the expense of more mouths to feed. By 1854, Palmer was heavily in debt because of gambling and he began forging his mother's signature on checks to pay off creditors. He took out a huge life insurance policy on his wife, Ann, and then she died under suspicious circumstances shortly afterward. She was only twenty-seven years old. He collected on her policy.

Still heavily in debt, with two creditors threatening to speak to his mother and thus exposing his fraud, Palmer attempted to take out life insurance on his brother, Walter. Walter was a drunk and soon became reliant on his brother, who readily plied him with several bottles of gin and brandy a day. Walter Palmer died in August 1855; however, the insurance company refused to pay up on the policy and instead sent inspectors to investigate. The investigators discovered that Palmer had been attempting to take out a substantial life insurance policy on George Bate, a farmer who worked briefly for Palmer. The investigators found that Bate was either misinformed or lying about the details of his insurance policy, and they informed Palmer that the company would not pay out on the death of his brother. They recommended a further inquiry into his brother's death. Palmer was then involved in an affair with Eliza Tharme, his housemaid. In June 1855, Tharme gave birth to the illegitimate son, increasing the financial burdens of the struggling physician.

Following John Cook's untimely and suspicious death, his stepfather, William Stevens, arrived on the scene to represent the family. Palmer informed Stevens that Cook had lost his betting books, which he further claimed were of no use as all bets were off once the gambler had died. He told Stevens that Cook had substantial outstanding gambling debts. Suspicious, Stevens requested an inquest into the death of his stepson. Palmer obtained a death certificate for Cook from an eighty-year-old, senile doctor who listed Cook's cause of death as apoplexy. A postmortem examination of Cook's body took place and was carried out by a medical student and his assistant, Charles Newton. Newton was drunk and Palmer interfered with the examination, bumping into Newton and taking the stomach contents off in a jar for safekeeping. The jars were sent off to be examined but because of the poor quality of the contents, a second postmortem was arranged.

Further investigation showed that the town's postmaster had intercepted a letter addressed to the coroner on behalf of Palmer. In the letter

Palmer requested that the verdict of death be given as natural causes and included a financial payment. Ironically, the postmaster who intercepted the letter was later prosecuted for interfering with the mail and was given two years in prison. Although no signs of poison were found during the autopsy, the jury at the inquest issued a finding that Cook had "died of poison willfully administered to him by William Palmer." Palmer was arrested on the charge of murder and forgery. A creditor told the police his suspicions that Palmer had been forging his mother's signature on various checks to pay off his gambling debts.

Palmer was held in jail where he threatened to go on a hunger strike but backed down when he was informed that this would lead to him being force fed. Through an act of Parliament, Palmer's trial was allowed to be held at the Old Bailey in London since a fair trial could not be held in Staffordshire, where detailed accounts of the Cook case and the deaths of his children were printed by local newspapers. The bodies of Ann, Palmer's wife, and Walter, Palmer's brother, were exhumed and re-examined. Some traces of lead poisoning were discovered in his wife's remains. The prosecution introduced forensic evidence and reliable witnesses. One witness for the defense, insurance agent Jeremiah Smith, insisted that he had no knowledge of Palmer taking out life insurance on his brother, Walter, despite Smith's signature being on the insurance form.

Circumstantial evidence also came to light. The chambermaid testified that as Cook was dying, he accused Palmer of murder. Another witness told the jury that he had seen Palmer purchasing strychnine. A chemist admitted selling Palmer strychnine in the belief that he was using it to poison a dog. He also admitted that he had failed to record the sale in his poison's book as required by law. Another chemist also admitted selling Palmer strychnine without noting the sale in his poison's book. Palmer's financial situation was also brought to light in the courtroom proceedings. A money lender told the court he lent money to Palmer at 60 percent interest, and Palmer's banker testified that Palmer's bank account was nearly empty.

The cause of Cook's death was hotly disputed, with each side bringing out medical witnesses. The eighty-year-old physician who had signed Cook's death certificate stated the cause of Cook's death was congestion of the brain. His testimony was dismissed by other physicians who claimed the doctor's judgment was clouded because he had become mentally feeble in his old age. The prosecution's medical witnesses testified that Cook's death was caused due to strychnine poisoning administered by Palmer. Palmer's attorney argued to the jury that no traces of poison had been found during the autopsy, summoning fifteen medical witnesses who stated that the poison should have been found in Cook's stomach, the contents of which had mysteriously disappeared during the autopsy when Palmer confiscated the material.

The prosecution painted a picture of Palmer to the jury as a man desperately in need of money in order to avoid debtor's prison, who murdered his friend for his money and who had covered his tracks by sabotaging the postmortem. The jury deliberated for just over an hour before returning a verdict of guilty. The judge ordered the death sentence. After the sensational trial, approximately 35,000 people turned out at prison in June 1856 to witness Palmer's hanging. As he stepped onto the gallows, Palmer is said to have looked at the trapdoor and exclaimed, "Are you sure it's safe?" Palmer was buried beside the prison chapel in a grave filled with quicklime. After he was hanged, his mother is reported to have said, "They have hanged my saintly Billy."

The salutation, "What's your poison?" is an idiomatic reference reportedly based on the events surrounding Palmer's murder trial.

Now, gentlemen, it is for you to say whether, upon a review of the whole of this evidence, you can come to any other conclusion than that the death of the deceased was occasioned by poison administered by the prisoner at the bar. Look to all this restless anxiety. It might possibly be compatible with innocence if it stood by itself alone; but you must remember that it is one of a series of things which, though small perhaps in their individual capacity, do, when grouped together, lead to the inevitable and irresistible conclusion that the prisoner was the cause of this man's death. This is the ease which you have to decide. You have in the prisoner a man laboring under a pressure almost overwhelming, with pecuniary liabilities which he is utterly unable to meet, involving penalties of the law which must bring down disaster and ruin upon him. The only mode by which he can prevent those consequences is by obtaining money; and under such circumstances we know that a comparatively small amount, if it will meet the exigencies of the moment and will avert the impending catastrophe of rain, will operate with immense power. You then find that he had access to the bedside of the man whose death you have now to inquire into. You find that he has means of administering poison to him, and that within 48 hours of the death he has twice acquired possession of the poison which we suppose him to have administered to the deceased. Then you have the death itself in its terrible and revolting circumstances, all of which are characteristic only of death by that poison—strychnine—and no other. You have then the fact that to the utmost of his ability the prisoner realizes the purpose for which it is suggested to you that the death was accomplished.

—WARD LOCK, *THE ILLUSTRATED AND UNABRIDGED EDITION OF THE TIMES REPORT OF THE TRIAL OF WILLIAM PALMER: FOR POISONING JOHN PARSONS COOK, AT RUGELEY,* 1856.

CHAPTER 10

The Loomis Gang

Wash Loomis, 1865

The infamous Loomis clan terrorized upstate New York counties for nearly sixty years. Wash Loomis, the leader of the Loomis clan, was killed by vigilantes in 1865, putting an end to the gang's reign of terror.

Following the violent and brutal murder of Wash Loomis in October 1865, it was difficult to discern who were the worse criminals— the infamous Loomis gang who terrorized upstate New York counties for nearly sixty years or the police vigilantes who killed him and put an end to the gang's reign of terror.

On the night of October 29, 1865, a band of vigilantes descended on the upstate New York home of Wash Loomis and his family. Inside Wash, his brothers and sisters, and several trusted men were all asleep. The vigilantes surrounded the house. One of the vigilantes knocked on the back door and called for Wash to come out. He woke the others and, armed with two revolvers, Wash went outside. It only took a matter of seconds before Loomis was hit over the head and disarmed. He was beaten severely by several of the men and shot. His body was found behind some barrels in the woodshed. A gunfight then erupted with men firing into the house and the Loomis gang firing back from within the house. No one, other than Wash Loomis, was injured in the melee.

Grove Loomis, who had rushed to his brother's defense, was the next victim. He was attacked and badly beaten, then covered with a blanket that was soaked in kerosene and set on fire. His sister, Cornelia, saved his life. Finding her brother locked in a back room, she managed to break in and douse the flames that engulfed Grove. Although he was beaten badly, she saved Grove from burning to death. The Loomis barn as well as the house was set on fire. The house was saved but the barn was burned to the ground and many valuable horses were killed.

After the attack, a coroner held an inquest over Wash's body. Grove Loomis swore it was County Sheriff James Filkins who had beaten Wash over the head and shot him, and that he was also the culprit who had beaten him and set him on fire. According to Grove's testimony, Filkins struck him on the head six or eight times as fast and as hard as he could. He also claimed he defended himself as well as he could but other vigilantes joined Filkins in the assault. Grove said Filkins also shot him. He said he fell to the floor and Filkins jumped on him two or three times, kicking him in the head and neck. Filkins then reportedly said, "Boys, he's dead. Let's burn him up." Cornelia also testified she saw Filkins inside the house attacking Grove.

The coroner's jury returned a verdict that, according to the testimony, Washington L. Loomis Jr. came to his death by the hands of three or more persons, and that one of these persons was James L. Filkins. Filkins agreed to turn himself into the authorities. In mid-November, Filkins appeared in court to face the charges against him, but no trial was held because the witnesses refused to appear in court.

The Loomis family had terrorized upstate New York counties for nearly sixty years. They robbed, rustled sheep and cattle, burned barns and homes, and even burnt down a county courthouse to hide evidence against them. The murder of Wash Loomis brought an end to the gang's stranglehold on the region.

The Loomis gang was led by George Washington Loomis Sr., who came to Oneida County in 1802, reportedly driven out of Vermont for horse stealing. He bought 385 acres of land in upstate New York and built a substantial farmhouse overlooking the Chenango Valley. In the valley was a nine-mile stretch of almost impenetrable cedar swamp where stolen horses, sheep, cattle, and other stolen loot were hidden and served as an always reliable escape route when the gang was pursued by the authorities. Two sisters and two brothers, Walter and Willard, later followed the elder Loomis to Oneida. Loomis and his wife Rhoda had ten children—four girls and six boys.

The Loomis farmhouse was spacious, and the family lived in style. The main table was always set with fine silverware and expensive plates, cups, and glasses. The table was always abounding with meat, fish, breads, and vegetables, most often stolen from neighboring farms. And there was always an abundance of alcohol. The best whiskey was as free as water. Day or night visitors would stop in to eat, drink, make merry, and discuss current events in the counties. Strangers and acquaintances alike were all were seemingly welcomed. Farmworkers lived in a row of old cabins on the opposite side of the road, toward the swamp. A grove of maples covered the steep brow of the hill and back of the house.

All the Loomis children were dressed in the finest, most fashionable clothes. The large family was indoctrinated to a life of crime at an early age. When the young sons were about to leave the house, Rhona Loomis advised them, "Now, don't come back without stealing something, if it's nothing but a jackknife."

The gang specialized in stealing horses and rustling livestock—sheep, hogs, and fowls—but they also dealt in fencing stolen goods, burglaries, and counterfeiting. Although the Loomis family was the core of the gang, it also included groups of young men from the area out to make a fast buck, as well as criminals from elsewhere. There were generally half a dozen young men who ran with the gang at any given time. The most of the thefts and barn-burning was done by these young men, while the Loomis family acted as the receivers of the stolen goods.

The Loomises were successful both in crime and in legitimate agriculture and were able to bribe local authorities, judges, and politicians for protection. And, for many years, they cultivated goodwill among their neighbors. When their neighbors suffered from thefts, those who went to the Loomis farm for help often received aid in recovering their property. This helped guarantee that the locals would not be willing to give evidence against the Loomis gang to outside authorities. Most people in the region were either in the Loomis's debt or afraid of them. Anybody who complained to the law about them frequently ran the risk of mysterious fires on their property or, worse, personal harm to them or their families.

According to Amos Cummings's newspaper article, appearing in the 1877 edition of *The New York Sun*, "They rule the counties of Oneida, Oswego, Otsego, Madison, Chenango, Schoharie, Delaware, and Sullivan with a rod of iron."

"They have numerous well-trained confederates in all of these counties, who are ready by day or night, at a moment's warning, to ride off in any direction for the sake of plundering or for the concealment or protection of associates who are in danger of falling into the meshes of the law," Cummings said.

"These men have been indicted times without number . . . but none of them have ever been convicted, nor have any of them been in jail for a longer time than was sufficient for a bondsman to arrive at prison," he said.

Of the six sons of George Washington Sr. and Rhonda Loomis, the second born, Wash, became the leader of the Loomis gang after his father's death in 1856 at seventy-one years old. The family was then left to their own devices and Wash stepped up to fill the void. The six sons included William W. Washington (Wash), Grove L. Wheeler, Amos Plumb, and Hiram Denio. The daughters included Calista, Charlotte, Cornelia, and Lucia. Among his brothers and sisters, Wash's word became law. Unusually bright and articulate, he was reportedly a keen observer of human nature, endowed with alluring personality that few could resist, and had a keen understanding of both sides of the law, having learned at his father's and mother's knees the ins and outs of their criminal empire, as well as briefly studying at a local law office. He was handsome, dashing, well dressed, and was a general favorite with men and women alike.

In 1848, Wash was forced to flee to California briefly prior to his father's death when he and others stormed a local barn dance, entered without paying, and insisted on dancing. It ended up in a bloody melee with several men badly injured. Wash was indicted for an assault with intent to kill. While being held, he was also charged with stealing a saddle and bridle. Although released on bail, he decided to jump bail rather than go to trial and ran off to California, where he stayed for several years. He returned from California before the death of his father. By then, those pressing charges against him had died and the original indictments against him were dropped.

In his absence and following his return, burglaries, cattle and sheep rustling, and a host of other petty crimes were a nightly occurrence. By 1856, the farmers in the region were weary of the Loomis clan and their outrage grew. They accused the family of various crimes but still nothing was done and no one was apprehended.

But the Loomis gang's luck began to run out when twenty-one-year-old blacksmith James Filkins became constable. He knew both the elder Loomis and Wash, having shod horses for them both. He even attended the elder Loomis's funeral but his relationship with Wash and the rest of the family changed in 1858 when he was elected the town constable of Brookfield in Madison County. By then the entire region was fed up with the Loomis thievery but frustrated that no law officers would serve warrants against any members of the family. Filkins, however, swore to bring the family to justice. It was a personally costly endeavor. He was nearly assassinated, shot three times, his family terrorized, his home nearly burnt to the ground, and he was indicted at least a half dozen times by corrupt grand juries on Wash Loomis's payroll. Still he persevered to the very end.

The robbing and thievery escalated under Wash's command. In one instance, one of the Loomis daughters, Cornelia, and several of her brothers attended a dance in Brookfield. Several of the women at the dance complained that their muffs had been stolen from the cloak room. Some of the stolen merchandize was later found at the Loomis home. Cornelia claimed ignorance and, since no one had seen her or her brothers steal the merchandize, no charges were filed.

In another brazen incident, a Brookfield rancher sold a yoke of cattle to someone for $160. The stranger who purchased them paid in cash. When the rancher went to the bank to deposit the money, the teller told the rancher the money was counterfeit. The rancher tracked the cattle to the Loomis farm where he found them grazing. When he confronted Wash and the others, they claimed to have bought them from the same stranger. As it turned out, the stranger who had bought the cattle from the rancher in the first place using the counterfeit money was Cornelia Loomis dressed in men's clothing. The robbery of the cattle incensed many residents but no effort to hold the Loomises accountable was undertaken. The rancher lost all his cattle.

In June 1858, a local farmer charged the Loomis clan with highway robbery for stealing his sheep. Filkins subsequently charged Wash, Grove, and Plumb Loomis with highway robbery, and they were indicted. Filkins was one of the constables who served the warrants on the Loomis clan on the charge of highway robbery. It was his first confrontation with the Loomis gang as a constable. It wouldn't be his last.

Filkins surrounded the Loomis house with seven men. Plumb tried to reach the swamp through the tall grass, but Filkins outran and captured him. Plumb was hysterical and Filkins threatened to beat him if he didn't quiet down. All the others at the house managed to escape except for Plumb. He was taken back to Brookfield and locked in a room at a local hotel to await trial. Shortly after the arrest, Grove Loomis showed up on horseback at the hotel with a gang of several men. He was brandishing several revolvers and demanded Plumb's release. Filkins stepped out onto the porch of the hotel holding a shotgun. Seeing the armed and determined constable, Grove thought better of his mission and rode off. That night Plumb was put to bed on the upper floor of the hotel, handcuffed to a deputy. The next morning, Plumb was gone. He had escaped out of a second-floor window. It was suspected that the deputy had either been bribed or threatened to let Plumb escape.

Filkins made so many attempts at arresting the Loomises, and so Wash and the others decided to punish him. They had tried everything else from bribery to threatening him and his family, but Filkins was the one thing Wash and his family could not understand—an honest man. Using their many political connections, Wash tried to have Filkins arrested for assault and battery but the warrant for Filkins's arrest was thrown out of court. The Loomises even took a case for attempted murder by Filkins to the Grand Jury claiming he had tried to shoot and kill Plumb and Wash. This too was thrown out of court.

Grove Loomis was indicted by the Grand Jury for passing counterfeit money. When word got out that the District Attorney prosecuting the case kept the counterfeit money in the pocket of his waist coat, he was suspiciously accosted on the street by a gang of ruffians who stole his coat and with it the counterfeit money that was to be used as evidence against Grove. Without it, there was no case against Loomis and so the charges were dropped.

The Loomises broke down the door to Filkins's home one evening shortly afterward and, waving arrest warrants, shackled Filkins and hauled him off to the local magistrate to be arraigned. Luckily, several of Filkins's friends had been keeping watch over the Filkins's homestead and followed the wagon to the magistrate's office. The magistrate set bail and his friends paid it. The case against Filkins never went to court.

Disgusted with the ongoing events and with the Loomis's control over the legal and political system in Madison County, Filkins moved to Oneida County but his reputation as an unflinching honest lawman preceded him and he was immediately nominated and elected as constable in that county. Filkins agreed to accept the position on the promise of the people of Oneida to support him in his efforts to end the Loomis's crime wave. When Plumb Loomis heard of Filkins's election, he swore that if

Filkins ever came on the Loomis premises to arrest him he'd shoot him. Plumb's threat did not deter Filkins, who went to the Loomis home and tried to serve Plumb with an arrest warrant for threatening a law officer. Plumb made an effort to escape but was caught, placed in jail but subsequently bailed.

The Loomis gang became even more brazen and more and more burglaries; petty thefts; and sheep, horse, and cattle rustling increased. People complained, but their complaints to the authorities were met with violent and fiery retribution. People taking out complaints against the Loomises soon found their barns and homesteads burned. The gang had become so bold, and had burned so many barns and homes belonging to those who had spoken up against them, that the residents of the county were terrified, and Filkins found it nearly impossible to raise a posse.

Still, Filkins served warrants on the Loomis family oftentimes riding there alone. By July 1863, dozens of indictments were issued against the Loomises but they always managed to escape trial. Finally, Wash Loomis had enough. At midnight on July 22, 1863, a gang of riders converged on Filkins' home. His wife was there taking care of a sick child. The riders shot through the window. Filkins was shot in the right arm and left hand. Two more shots were fired through the bedroom window. According to reports, "The blinds were shattered, and the lower part of the sash torn out. The bedroom door was filled with buckshot, and there were fourteen shot holes in the mantel. Seven buckshot and forty small shot had riddled the bed curtains." The gunshots aroused neighbors who rushed to the Filkins's home as the assailants rode off.

In late September 1864, the Loomis gang pulled off its most brazen crime. The gang burned down the courthouse located in Madison County where dozens of indictments against the family had been filed and stored. Thinking they had rid themselves of all the indictments, they discovered that the indictments had been removed from the courthouse and were instead being kept at office of the County Clerk in a fireproof building in Morrisville. A week after the courthouse was burned to the ground, the gang broke into the clerk's offices, found the indictments, and burned them all in a stove. Every indictment against the family was destroyed. New indictments against them were never issued.

After the destruction of the courthouse and the indictments, the Loomis gang viewed themselves as untouchable by the law and this was perhaps their ultimate undoing. The destruction of the indictments bolstered the gang. Robberies and rustling became a nightly occurrence, with the gang reaching into other counties throughout the region. Finally, a secret meeting was held at a North Brookfield Church where a group of farmers, ranchers, and other citizens gathered to organize a citizens' group determined to rid the region of the gang, one way or another. When Wash Loomis got wind of the meeting, he and a group of his men showed up at the church and quickly dispersed the gathering.

The group met again in secret, this time determined to find a way to end the Loomis's reign of terror. If the gang was willing to burn courthouses and clerk's offices in order to maintain their control, there was no telling what they might resort to. And if the law could not protect them, they decided to find a way to protect themselves outside the law. Filkins, who had been shot twice, his home nearly burned to the ground, his wife and family terrorized, and his life put in daily danger could hardly argue against the group's decision.

In October 1865, vigilantes attacked the Loomis compound, killed Wash Loomis, and critically injured Grove. Filkins was charged with the crime but no trial was held.

Following Wash's murder, there were several unsuccessful attempts on Filkins's life. While serving a warrant on the Loomis home, he and his deputies were met with a fusillade of gunfire from several men holed up inside the house. Filkins was shot in the arm, but the deputies were able to disarm those inside the house and haul them to jail.

The Loomis gang tried to carry on as they had previously, but people lost their fear of them. Other vigilante gangs were organized, and in 1866, another mob attacked the Loomis home and burned it to the ground, including everything in it. Plumb Loomis was hung to a tree and would have died if his sister, Cornelia, hadn't begged for his life. After the incident, the gang fell apart and their stranglehold over the upstate New York counties ended. But their infamous legend still lives on in the annals of American crime.

Following the burning down of their home, the Loomis clan fled to the four winds, with Plumb retiring to a small farm near the Canadian border and Grove disappearing into obscurity. Cornelia Loomis lived out the rest of her life in Hastings, New York. The family ultimately lost their farm to tax arrears and it was auctioned off. Cornelia Loomis died in 1893. Grove Loomis died in 1877. Plumb Loomis died in 1903, and James Filkins died in 1893 at sixty-eight years old.

The operations of this ruffian [Grove Loomis] and the daring and intrepidity he exhibits in avoiding the officers, are startling and wonderful. He lives among his followers and courtesans, in Sangerfield, like Robin Hood in Sherwood Forest. Members of the gang venture out to prey on society at pleasure, and return to their stronghold, like knights of the black-hand, in the unsettled days of the Scotch border. Indictments and bench warrants amount to little more than waste paper; for a system of spies and defense has been organized, that gives them warning of the approach of officers, and the Loomises seem to delight in narrow escapes and triumph over the bands that come to arrest them. Grove Loomis, like the Scotch Wallace is a match for all who come against him; and is unfailing in resources and prompt in their use, as was ever the patriot trooper Marion.
—THE UTICA ONEIDA WEEKLY, NOVEMBER 21, 1858

The house of Mr. Filkins, in North Brookfield, was entered on Tuesday night of this week, by a gang of what is known as the "Loomis tribe." Filkins, after being badly beaten, was, in a bruised and bleeding condition, shackled and carried over to the swamp, since which, up to going to press, nothing has been heard from him. The case is greatly aggravated by the fact that access to Filkins' house was obtained through the base treachery of a pretended friend, one Kit Mason.
—THE WATERVILLE TIMES, MAY 10, 1861

I was awakened by Mr. Filkins rapping on the door of my room and calling me this was about two o'clock [in the morning]. It was Filkins voice he said he wanted to see me. . . . Mr. Filkins was standing close to the door he did not say what he wanted; he took me by the collar. I said, "I will go with you Mr. Filkins" he said, "I know you will" and handed me rather roughly . . . three men were standing near the head of the chamber stairs they stepped aside and let us go down they had guns in their hands. Filkins also had a gun but had a lighted candle on a candlestick in his left hand. One of the others I think had a Lantern. . . . I said "let me see Washington for a moment" as we were nearby his bedroom. I started to go towards the door, and he pulled me back by the collar roughly and said to me, "he is not there come with me and I will take care of you." We all walked into the back kitchen and the others followed. . . . Filkins walked over . . . to my overcoat which was hanging up near the door and felt in the pockets and said "Now where are my handcuffs" I said "Mr. Filkins you don't need any handcuffs I will go with you," he said "I think you will." . . . Instantly he struck me six or eight times in the head as fast and as hard as he could. I staggered against the side of the room. . . . They then struck me two or three times. I did not fall until he struck me five or eight times with a sling shot. He had a revolver which he fired at me which missed me. . . . He then struck me with the revolver and broke his revolver in two. I then fell and he kicked me two or three times on the side of the stomach and the others I think kicked me at the same time on the head and neck. Filkins then said, "plum he is dead let's burn him up." At this he . . . threw on some kerosene or something out of a bottle over me and set fire to it. It burned very quick. They then went out the door into the woodhouse I saw nothing more then.

—*THE UTICA DAILY OBSERVER*, NOVEMBER 3, 1865
(THE TESTIMONY OF GROVE LOOMIS AT COURT):

CHAPTER 11

Bad Bridget

Bridget Durgan, 1867

In a fit of jealousy, Irish immigrant Bridget Durgan murdered her employer, Mary Ellen Coriell, stabbing her twenty-three times.

In a fit of frenzy, Irish maid Bridget Durgan murdered her employer, Mary Ellen Coriell, by stabbing her twenty-three times in the hopes of becoming her widowed husband's new wife but the only aisle she ended up walking was the aisle to the gallows.

AROUND 1:00 A.M. ON THE MORNING OF FEBRUARY 26, 1867, ISRAEL Coriell, of Newmarket, New Jersey, was awakened by someone desperately knocking on his front door. When he opened the door, he saw it was Bridget Durgan, a young servant girl of his cousin, Dr. Lester Wallace Coriell. She had the doctor's two-year-old daughter, Mamey, in her arm. Durgan was hysterical. She told him burglars were ransacking the doctor's house while the doctor was out on a medical call. She said she feared that the doctor's wife, Mary Ellen, was being murdered.

Coriell sent her to awaken his neighbor, Reverend William Little, while he ran to Main Street and rang a large bell as a signal of general alarm. Reverend Little and two other men followed Durgan back to Dr. Coriell's house. They discovered the house was filled with smoke and uncovered a smoldering fire in one of the bedrooms. They doused the fire and to their horror found there were signs of a fearful struggle in the room. Clothing was strewn in piles and feathers ripped from the pillows were scattered on the floor, all drenched with blood and gore.

A broken chair in the room was broken to pieces and covered with blood. In the middle of the room lay the body of Mary Ellen Coriell. Her body covered from her forehead to her breasts with hideous stab wounds. Authorities later determined she had been stabbed twenty-three times. Her jugular vein had been ripped out, and there were four deep teeth marks in her neck.

When Durgan was questioned, she said two men had called at around 8:30 p.m. looking for the doctor and they were told that he was visiting a patient. According to Durgan, they left but then they returned two hours later and Mrs. Coriell let them in to wait for the doctor to return. Soon after, she heard Mrs. Coriell scream and then called to her telling her to take the child and go for the doctor. Bridget picked up the baby and hurried to Israel Coriell's house. Information about the gruesome crime was telegraphed to police departments in New Jersey and New York.

The next day as detectives looked for the murderers, a coroner's jury was empaneled and began examining witnesses. The knife used in the murder was found in the downstairs bathroom. It had come from the Coriell's kitchen. Durgan claimed she knew the two men who had come to the house that evening and identified them as Barney Doyle and John Hunt. She said both men had a grudge against Dr. Coriell over the treatment he had given to their family members. Doyle and Hunt were apprehended and brought into court. Although Durgan had identified them as the men who had come to the house the night before, both men had alibis and witnesses to back them up.

Hearing the news, Durgan quickly changed her story. She told the court that a servant girl named Anne Linnen had killed Mrs. Coriell during an attempted robbery of the house. According to Durgan, Linnen took the butcher knife from the kitchen and went into the sitting room where Mrs. Coriell was sleeping and said, "An American woman's life ain't worth anything anyhow." But when Linnen was brought before the court, she too had an airtight alibi. Soon enough Durgan was under suspicion.

Dr. Coriell testified that his wife had been dissatisfied with Durgan's work, and fired her shortly before the murder. Durgan was supposed to have left the household on February 22, but she had taken sick, and the Coriells let her stay until she regained her health.

Another witness testified that she had seen Durgan changing her clothes in the yard shortly after the murder. The teeth marks on the victim's neck were compared to Durgan and were found to correspond exactly. When it became clear to her that she was now the prime suspect in the murder, she sprang up, striking the table with her fist and crying out, "Who'll dare swear I did the murder? You've all questioned me and think I did it. What else do you want to know? I know how did it, but I won't tell you." The coroner's jury deliberated for fifteen minutes and then charged Durgan with the willful and brutal murder of Mrs. Coriell.

Durgan was a stout Irish girl who had been in America for two years and had worked for the Coriell family for four months. Her features were plain and unexpressive and she had drooping eyelids giving her face a somewhat evil look. The newspapers were not sure what to make of her. *The New York Herald* wrote, "Her manner throughout the inquest yesterday betokened that she was either a cunning evil doer, hiding her moral ugliness under a simulated appearance of a half idiot, or a half-witted creature in the full sense of the word."

The case went to trial on May 20. The courtroom was filled to capacity and many spectators were turned away due to lack of space. The trial lasted eleven days, and more than seventy witnesses testified, but there was very little information that was not included in the inquest. Durgan continued to maintain that the murder was committed by the two men who came to the house earlier in the evening and her attorney asserted that nothing in the testimony contradicted this. He claimed that it would have been impossible for Durgan to have committed the deed without being drenched with blood.

The prosecution presented a compelling case of circumstantial evidence, giving much weight to the marks on the neck but stating, "It was not the single link, but the continuous chain of facts which bound the prisoner to the scene through all its bloody details with links of iron and hooks of steel." The jury took only twenty minutes to return a verdict of guilty of murder in the first degree. When the judge sentenced Bridget Durgan to be hanged, many in the gallery applauded.

The date of the execution was set for August 30, and while awaiting execution in prison, Durgan wrote three separate confessions. Each was contradictory. Many continued to believe that she had not acted alone and was protecting someone else. Mary Gilroy who had testified for the defense was a known pickpocket who had been a friend of Durgan's in New York was questioned after the trial and was held as a possible accomplice.

Durgan's fourth confession, given the day before her execution, was the most complete. She said she acted alone and that Mary Gilroy was absolutely innocent. The motive, she said, was not robbery as most believed, but to remove Mrs. Coriell so that she could take her place as the doctor's wife. She wrote, "It came into my head that if Mrs. Coriel were only out of the way, that I would have a very good place with the Doctor, as he would no doubt still keep house and have me take care of it and Mamey (the Coriels' baby) who was fond of me. This brought Mrs. Horning into my mind, and instantly, like a flash of lightning, I felt impelled to kill Mrs. Coreil." She stated that when she heard that the doctor was going away, she put the butcher knife in a convenient place and she described in gruesome detail how she had committed the murder and set fire to the house.

Durgan's life had been a series of brutal events. She was a twenty-two-year-old illiterate, indigent immigrant from County Sligo, Ireland, who was essentially exported from Ireland by wealthy, British landowners who saw the poor and uneducated as an economic burden. She was shipped to Liverpool in 1866, then to New York City only a few months before she was hanged. In fact, she had spent the earliest years of her life in dire poverty, living near starvation on farmland infected by the potato fungus.

By the age of ten, she was helping her father unload barges along Killala Bay, living as a gypsy, eating cabbage, and sleeping in barns or warehouses. Finally, after her father's lungs began to fail, the family sought refuge at Union Poor Law workhouses in Sligo.

Ultimately, they were admitted to the workhouse at Carrick-on-Shannon in County Leitrim, where she watched her family waste away from lung, bone, and joint tuberculosis.

Bridget's mother, sister, and two brothers died of tuberculosis in 1865 in Carrick-on-Shannon. They were buried in unmarked graves in the long furrows of loose earth behind the workhouse infirmary.

While previously living in New York City and not able to find work, Durgan became a prostitute. She became pregnant and gave up the baby. She then fled to Brooklyn and went into domestic service. Her employer, Mrs. Mary Horning, soon hated her. Finally, Mrs. Horning called her "a devilish infernal slut" and fired her. Durgan vowed to kill the woman and might have if not for the woman's husband who threw Durgan out of his house. She was determined to kill Horning and sent her poisoned cakes and stalked her outside her house with a knife. The authorities soon put an end to it when Horning contacted them about her behavior.

In 1867, most people in New Jersey and the surrounding states believed that Durgan was a brutish woman, little more than an animal, who had willfully and violently murdered her employer for financial and personal gain. People believed this because that's what the newspapers printed. The story had all the makings of good crime drama, including the genteel doctor's wife and mother of a beautiful daughter murdered by an ignorant, immigrant housemaid and former prostitute. Mrs. Coriell was described as "being possessed of the greatest beauty" and "a tender and noble heart," compared to Bridget who was a "demon girl" and "wicked creature." Within hours of her employer's murder, multiple newspapers published Bridget's "confession" and described her as an immigrant "fiend" and a "wild beast," portrayals that increased newspaper sales and interest in the case.

While in prison, many people came to see Bridget and tickets were also sold to attend her execution. One of the many visitors to her cell was the writer and women's activist and poet Elizabeth Oakes Smith, then entering her seventh decade. It was, she said, a habit of hers to "visit the prisons . . . that I may the better understand my own sex in every aspect." Her visit to Durgan resulted in an article detailing their meeting. The article was far from flattering. Smith compared parts of Durgan's appearance to that of various animals, as well as stating that her hands are "large, coarse, and somehow have a dangerous look, for hands, as well as faces, have expression."

Smith published the article in *The New York Times* and wrote, "In the scale of human intelligence I find Bridget Durgin [*sic*] on the very lowest level. She has cunning and ability to conceal her real actions; and so have the fox, the panther, and many inferior animals, whose instincts are not more clearly defined than those of Bridget Durgin."

A booklet published shortly after Durgan's execution supposedly giving an account of her life stated, "Throughout all the annals of crime, there has never been recorded a more revolting, wicked deed, than that for which the wretched perpetrator, Bridget Durgan, paid the forfeit of her life in the jail yard of New Brunswick, New Jersey, on August 30, 1867."

George Maxwell Robeson served as the attorney general who successfully prosecuted the case against Durgan. Robeson was able to gain a conviction on circumstantial evidence. Robeson argued that, despite the lack of forensic science, blood on Durgan's dress was the blood of Mrs. Coriell. He told the jury not to consider Durgan was a woman when making a verdict. Throughout Robeson's closing arguments, Durgan held her head low and constantly had a handkerchief to her eyes. Robeson was applauded by the courtroom audience after he finished giving his closing arguments. Interest in the execution was intense. On August 30, the Third Regiment of the New Jersey Rifle Corps was mobilized to surround the courthouse in New Brunswick where the hanging was to take place. The Sheriff of Middlesex County, J. Manning Clarkson, had hoped to limit witnesses to 200 people but that number soon swelled to 500. New Jersey state law required executions to be private, prohibiting admittance to anyone but the sheriff, his deputies, and other specified officials, and so, in compliance with the law, Sheriff Clarkson deputized all 500 witnesses. Durgan was accompanied on the scaffold by two Catholic priests. According to reports, while the priests were whispering in her ear, the rope was cut and "after an almost imperceptible quiver, Bridget Durgan was no more!"

> She is large in the base of the brain, and swells out over the ears, where destructiveness and secretiveness are located by phrenologists, while the whole region of intellect, ideality and moral sentiment is small. . . . The character of Bridget's face is sullen, and yet wears a mixed expression of anxiety, even to distress. The line of the mouth, as of the eyelids, is oblique. There is not one character of beauty, even in the lowest degree, about the girl; no one ray of sentiment, nothing genuine, hardly human, except a weak, sometimes a bitter, smile. The wonder is that any housekeeper should be willing to engage such a servant. I have an idea that this same girl was offered to me in an intelligence office in Brooklyn, and that I refused to even talk to one so repulsive in appearance.
>
> —REVEREND BRENDAN, *LIFE, CRIMES, AND CONFESSION OF BRIDGET DURGAN. THE FIENDISH MURDERESS OF MRS. CORIELL; WHOM SHE BUTCHERED HOPING TO TAKE HER PLACE IN THE AFFECTIONS OF THE HUSBAND OF HER INNOCENT AND LOVELY VICTIM. THE ONLY AUTHENTIC, AND HITHERTO UNPUBLISHED HISTORY OF HER WHOLE LIFE; AND THE HIDEOUS CRIME FOR WHICH SHE WAS EXECUTED AT NEW BRUNSWICK, N. J., 1867.*

Finally I concluded that the time had come for the accomplishment of my wicked purpose, and putting away my sewing, I got ready. By this time my mistress was fast asleep, and, in order not to awaken her I pulled off my shoes. I then got out my butcher knife, and examined It well, to see that it would do its bloody work surely. Then clenching it firmly in my right hand, and, gritting my teeth together, I stepped as lightly as a cat into the room where my intended victim was lying on the lounge. . . . I was afraid that Mrs. Coriel would wake up and see me, and my desire was to kill her instantly in her sleep, before she could get her eyes open; for I had read in the paper of a murder in Italy, or somewhere else where the likeness of the murderer was fixed upon the retina of the murdered man's eye. My idea was to take good aim at her heart, give her a stab and roll her on to the floor, with her face down, so that she could not see me. However, I could not wait to steady myself; and so I plunged the butcher knife into the body of Mrs, Coriel, taking as good an aim as possible at her heart! She clutched me by the throat with one hand, and, seizing the knife in the other, she almost got it away from me. Then we rolled about the floor each of us trying to get the mastery, when, losing my knife, I endeavored to kill her by biting her neck; as I used to do when killing a chicken for cooking.
—Bridget Durgan, "Confession," 1867.

CHAPTER 12

Bring Back Our Darling

William Mosher and Joseph Douglas, 1874

CHARLEY ROSS.

Four-year-old Charley Ross was kidnapped from the front yard of his Philadelphia home on July 1, 1874, in the first kidnapping for ransom case. The kidnappers of Charley Ross were never apprehended and the boy was never found.

Four-year-old Charley Ross was kidnapped from the front yard of his Philadelphia home on July 1, 1874, and his father began the search for his son that would last until his death in 1897.

The young Ross brothers, four-year-old Charley and his six-year-old brother, Walter, were playing in the front yard of their attractive, three-story, stone house located on East Washington Lane, in the Philadelphia suburb of Germantown. The two were constant companions and seldom went anywhere without each other. They were the children of wealthy Philadelphia grocer Christian Ross and his wife, Sarah Anne. Along with Charley and Walter, the Rosses had five other children: Stroughton, Harry, Sophia, Marian, and Annie. Charley, whose given name was Charles Brewster Ross, was a cherubic young child with long flaxen curls. Always smiling, his friendly nature made him a favorite with everyone who met him.

It was July 1, 1874, and the boys, along with the rest of the city, were looking forward to the upcoming Fourth of July celebration. Walter saw a familiar horse and buggy coming up the street with two men at the reins. He hoped it was the same two men who had given him and his brother candy on the previous Saturday. On June 27, 1874, the two men drove by the Ross home and seeing Charley and Walter playing on the sidewalk nearby, they stopped, and offered the two boys candy while they engaged them in idle conversation. The two men drove by each day afterward, always stopping and speaking with the two boys. It was the same two men who approached the boys on this particular afternoon and both boys were excited to see them hoping they would once again give them candy. According to Walter, it was Charley who asked them for a ride and also asked them to purchase him candy and firecrackers to celebrate the upcoming Fourth of July. The two strangers agreed and Charley and Walter climbed into the buggy. At the time, Charley's mother and several of his siblings were in Atlantic City where she was recovering from an unnamed illness. The boys' father thought they were playing in a neighbor's yard.

As the buggy ambled off down the road for a short distance, Charley asked why they didn't stop at some store to buy the candy and fireworks as they had promised. The men told him that they would go to a general store up the road, "Aunt Susie's," on the corner of Palmer and Richmond streets where they would buy them whatever they wanted. This seemed to appease Charley. When they reached store, Walter was given 25 cents and told to go into the store, and fill up on candy and fireworks. Walter dutifully followed their instructions and went inside. While Walter was inside making his purchases, the kidnapers drove off with Charley.

When Walter came out of the store, he began crying when he realized that he had been abandoned and that the men and Charley were gone. A store patron, finding Walter sobbing outside the store, managed to get Walter to tell him what happened and took the boy back to his home. During the subsequent investigation, several people came forward who testified they had seen the buggy drive pass them with both boys in it, but no one came forward who saw the buggy drive off with only Charley on board. The tragic chain of events was just beginning.

On July 4, 1874, Christian Ross received the first of the ransom notes, demanding $20,000 for the safe return of his son, Charley. The ransom note, including all the misspellings, read:

> Be not uneasy you son Charley Bruster be all writ we's him and no powers on earth can deliver out of our hand. You will have to pay us before you git him from us, and pay us a big cent too. If you put the cops hunting for him yu is only defeting yu own end. We is got him put so no living power gets him from us a live. If any aproch is maid to his hiding place tha is the signil for his instant annihilition. If yu regard his lif puts no one to search for him yu can fetch him out alive and no other existin powers. Don't deceive yuself and think the detectives ca git him from us for that is imposebel. Yu here from us in a few days.

The way the kidnappers demanded to communicate with the Ross family was writing messages in the personal section of the *Philadelphia Ledger* newspaper. The initial ransom note told Mr. Ross to communicate with the kidnappers in the newspaper. He was told to published the following communique: "Ros. we are ready to negotiate."

On July 7, Ross replied as directed, and on the same day, another letter was mailed to him in which he was directed to state in a personal whether or not he would come to terms.

At the direction of the police, it was decided to continue answering the letters but to respond as ambiguously as possible in order to keep the communications going. The police hoped that by keeping the communications between Ross and the kidnappers ongoing, the kidnappers would eventually slip up and reveal something that would help the authorities apprehend them and help bring back Charley.

Ross continued his newspaper correspondence with the kidnappers. "Ros will come to terms to the best of his ability," he published in the newspaper. On July 9, another letter was sent to Ross stating the kidnappers were growing impatient and that the reason for the evasive answer was obvious to them. Despite the message from the kidnappers, Ross continued to publish ambiguous answers and later announced that he would not compound a felony by paying money to the monsters who committed this atrocious crime. But when Ross noted the mental and physical condition of his ailing wife, he regretted his position and immediately reopened negotiations with the kidnappers through the personal columns of the *Ledger*. Ultimately, the kidnappers exchanged twenty-three letters with the Ross family.

According to Patterson Smith, writing in *AB Bookmans' Weekly* in 1990, "It is generally agreed that the first American kidnaping for ransom took place on July 1, 1874, in the Germantown section of Philadelphia." The kidnapping was the year's most sensational story. It generated news stories throughout the country and became the first widely publicized kidnap-for-ransom affair.

Thousands of police, investigators, everyday men, women, and children became involved in the search for Charley Ross. The story of the kidnapping and subsequent efforts to find the child spread across the nation. In Europe, people were shocked at the crime. Kidnapping was so unheard of at the time that there were no laws to cover it. The case dragged on throughout the summer and fall, with every lead and tiny clue checked out. It was a tedious and frustrating task. People reported seeing what they thought was the lost child, but each lead proved to be wrong. Men with little boys were stopped and questioned around the world. The outrage generated by the crime became so overwhelming that in many instances the authorities set aside individual civil rights in favor of expediency and searched people and private properties without the proper legal authority. Those who protested the breach of their rights were viewed with suspicion. Parents, especially those of the wealthy class, became so fearful that they virtually made prisoners of their children. On July 22, Mayor William Stokley of Philadelphia offered a reward of $20,000 for the arrest of the kidnappers.

In late July, the kidnappers instructed Ross to get a suitcase and, after painting it white, to put $20,000 in small bills inside and take the train leaving at midnight for New York City. He was instructed to stand on the rear platform of the last car. This train was due to arrive in about one hour after sunrise. Ross was told to be on the alert from the moment the train left the depot, and if he saw a torch and a white flag waved at nighttime near the track or a white flag alone in the day time, he should throw the suitcase with the money off the train immediately. If and when the kidnappers found it and all the money inside it was accounted for, the child would be returned home within the next twenty-four hours.

Ross followed all the instructions save one—instead of placing the $20,000 inside the suitcase, he placed a letter in which he stated that he would not pay the money until he saw his son alive. He took his position on the rear car of the train and made the journey as he had been instructed but he never saw any signal from the kidnappers, neither a torch nor a white flag. Seeing no signal from the kidnappers, he returned home. Shortly afterward, he received a letter from the kidnappers reprimanding him for not making the trip. The letter had been mailed from New York City. The kidnappers stated that the simultaneous exchange was impossible and they again threatened to kill the child if Ross didn't comply fully to their specific demands.

On August 2, Chief of Police George Walling of New York City contacted the Philadelphia authorities requesting the original letters from the kidnapers. He maintained that he had an informant with reliable information regarding the identity of the culprits. The Philadelphia police proceeded to New York with the necessary papers and Chief Walling's informant identified the writing as that of William Mosher, a known criminal. The informant told the New York police that in April 1874, Mosher and another known criminal, Joseph Douglas, tried to persuade him to join in the kidnapping of one of the wealthy Vanderbilt children while the child was playing on the lawn surrounding the family residence at Throgsneck, Long Island.

The child was to be held until a ransom of $50,000 was obtained, and the informant's part of the plot would be to take the child on a small launch and keep the boy in seclusion until the money was received, but he declined to enter into the conspiracy. He gave a complete physical description of the two men. The description was then relayed to Walter Ross who confirmed the description of the two men as the same two that had taken him and his brother.

Mosher was a boatbuilder by trade and a fugitive from the law at the time. In 1871, he was arrested for burglary at Freehold, New Jersey, but escaped from jail before his trial. At the time of the Charley Ross kidnapping, Mosher lived with his wife and four children on Monroe Street, Philadelphia, and Douglas lived with him. They reportedly kept their horse and buggy in a local stable, but the stable was torn down and the horse and buggy, which was undoubtedly the one in which Charley Ross was carried away, disappeared about the time of the kidnapping. In August, Douglas and Mosher and his family moved to New York, where Mosher had a brother-in-law named William Westervelt, who was formerly a police officer in that city.

The Pinkerton Detective Agency was called into the Charley Ross case and every effort was made to apprehend the two men, but by November, they had not been located. The Pinkertons issued a three-page circular with a photograph of the boy and offered a reward of $20,000. In September, the Pinkertons made a much broader distribution of a single-sheet reward flyer. The flyer generated thousands of false leads from around country but even the Pinkertons were unable to locate the two suspects. A song, "Bring Back Our Darling," about the missing child, was published in sheet-music form. Its last verse began: "O Father in Heaven, please hear Thou our pray'r!/Pray soften the hearts of those men/Who robbed us of one who is dearer than all/To bring back our darling again."

In early November, Ross, who had been in constant communication with the kidnapers, answered their twenty-third and last letter, which instructed him to send two relatives to New York City with the money and to stay in a particular hotel where they would be contacted by the abductors. He was told to announce two days in advance, through the personal column of *The New York Herald*, when they were coming. The message was to read: "Saul of Tarsus. Fifth Ave. Hotel—instant." They also warned Ross to instruct his relatives not to leave their room in the hotel on that day. The kidnappers explained that the person calling for the money at the hotel knew nothing about the affair and under no circumstances should the relatives speak with the him. They said that the route the messenger would take with the money had been carefully planned so that it would be impossible for him to be followed without them knowing it, and if he was followed, they would kill Charley. They assured him that if he did as they instructed, the child would be returned safely. It appeared they had thought of everything. Ross had no choice but to comply. He placed the notice in the *Herald* as instructed and sent his wife's brother and a nephew to New York City with $20,000. They stayed at the hotel they were instructed to, but no one came to claim it. This was the last time the kidnappers tried to negotiate with Ross.

The quest to locate Charley and the kidnappers came to an abrupt end during a failed burglary attempt on December 14, 1874, at the home of wealthy New Yorker Holmes Van Brunt, on the east side of New York. Van Brunt occupied his permanent home there and his brother lived next door, although he was not home at the time and the house was unoccupied. At 2 o'clock in the morning, the alarm bells in the unoccupied home of his brother began to ring arousing the family. Van Brunt directed his son, Albert, to go next door and investigate. The son had gone only a few feet outside when he saw someone in his uncle's home with a lighted candle. He ran back to his home and told his father. In the meantime, men who worked for Van Brunt, William Scott and Herman Frank, were aroused. The four men grabbed shotguns and revolvers and went to the house next door. Two men were stationed at the front entrance and two at the rear.

It was a cold, dark, rainy night, but the men waited patiently for nearly an hour. Finally, the dark forms of two men were seen as they quietly crept up out of the cellar in the rear of the house. Van Brunt ordered the two men to stop but his orders were met by gunfire. No one was hit. Van Brunt then emptied the contents of his shotgun into the first burglar who fell to the ground crying in pain. The second man fired at Van Brunt and attempted to escape by running to the front of the house where he was met by Van Brunt's son Albert. The two men exchanged gunfire but Albert was the better shot and the second burglar fell to the ground dead. The two men who were shot to death were Joseph Douglas and William Mosher.

Not knowing that his partner in crime was already dead, Douglas confessed to the Charley Ross kidnapping. "Men, I won't lie to you. My name is. Joseph Douglas and the man over there is William Mosher. He lives in New York, and I have no home. I am a single man and have no relatives except a brother and sister whom I have not seen for twelve years. Mosher is married and has four children. I have forty dollars in my pocket that I made honestly. Bury me with that," Douglas said.

"Men, I am dying now and it's no use lying. Mosher and I stole Charley Ross," he said.

When he was asked why he stole the child and he said, "To make money."

"Mosher knows all about the boy, ask him," he said.

Van Brunt and the others told him that Mosher was dead, and to prove it they dragged Mosher's body over to where Douglas could see it. "God help his poor wife and family," he managed to whisper. "Chief Walling knows all about us and was after us, and now he has us. The child will be returned home safe and sound in a few days."

Douglas slipped into unconsciousness and died without giving any further information about Charley Ross's whereabouts. The local authorities were contacted as well as Chief Walling in New York City. Walling sent a police detective who had known both Mosher and Douglas since childhood to identify the bodies. The detective recognized them immediately.

Young Walter Ross was sent to New York City where the bodies of Douglas and Mosher had been taken and when he was shown the bodies, he recognized them as the two men who drove the wagon and abducted them. Another eyewitness who saw the children in the buggy with the men also identified the remains. Mosher's widow was located and, while she admitted that she was aware of the fact that her husband kidnapped Charley Ross, she insisted that she did not know where he was concealed. Mr. Ross issued a circular that stated that, since the perpetrators of the kidnapping had been killed, he had no desire to prosecute the parties who still had his son. He stated he would give a $5,000 reward to any person who would return his son, no questions asked. This proved futile as well.

In February 1875, the Pennsylvania Legislature passed a law defining the offense of kidnapping and fixed the punishment at a fine not to exceed $10,000 and solitary confinement not to exceed twenty-five years, but it was specially provided that if any persons having any kidnapped child in their possession and who then returned the child unharmed would not be prosecuted.

For much of his life, Mr. Ross believed that his son was still alive because of the information he received from William Westervelt, Mosher's brother-in-law. He told Ross that he (Westervelt) had talked with Douglas the day before his death. Douglas told Westervelt that Mosher was making plans for the exchange of the child for the ransom. Although Ross believed Westervelt, Police Chief Walling repeatedly professed that he had conclusive evidence that the ex-policeman was aiding the kidnappers rather than the authorities. Walling had brought Westervelt into the investigation on an informal and confidential basis, while keeping his own detectives on the case. Westervelt's job was to attempt to locate the burglars through his sister. Day after day passed while Westervelt supposedly sought out Mosher and Douglas, whose whereabouts always seemed to elude him.

Walling began to wonder whether Westervelt was dutifully tracing the suspects or warning them about the policemen's own efforts. With the supposed kidnappers dead and no sign of Charley, the police turned their attention on Westervelt. The authorities were convinced of his complicity in the crime—if not in its actual commission, at least in shielding the kidnapers afterward. The ex-policeman was brought to trial in Philadelphia in August 1875, convicted on several counts of conspiracy in the kidnapping, and sentenced to seven years in prison.

The Ross family spent $60,000 searching for Charley, but to no avail. When the money ran out, Mr. Ross wrote a book about the kidnaping. The book, *The Father's Story of Charley Ross, the Kidnapped Child,* was published in 1876. Although it sold well, its profits were spent in Ross's search for his son. A related effort to publicize Charley's kidnapping entailed a Charley Ross glass bottle, which bore the boy's name and image. Although both these endeavors stimulated many alleged sightings of the child across the nation and even overseas, they were all proven false. Over the years, numerous people claiming to be Charley Ross came forward but all were refuted.

Christian Ross spent the rest of his life looking for his son. He traveled all over the United States and sometimes even out of the country following leads in the case. He died in 1897. After his death, his wife and Charley's brother, Walter, carried on the search, but the boy was never found. Sarah Anne Ross died in 1912 and her son, Walter, who had managed to escape the clutches of the kidnappers, died in 1943.

Mr. Ross– be not uneasy you son charly bruster he al writ we as got him and no powers on earth can deliver out of our hand. You wil hav two pay us befor you git him from us. an pay us a big cent to. if you put the cops hunting for him yu is only defeeting yu own end. we is got him fitt so no living power can gits him from us a live. if any aproch is maid to his hidin place that is the signil for his instant anihilation. if yu regard his lif puts no one to search for him you money can fech him out alive an no other existin powers don't deceve yuself and think the detectives can git him from us for that is one imposebel yu here from us in few day.

—First ransom note received July 3, 1874
[original spelling]

This is the lever that moved the rock that hides him from yu $20,000. Not one doler les—impossible—impossible—you cannot get him without it.

—Second ransom note received July 7, 1874
[original spelling]

The letter was then read aloud. So overwhelming was the astonishment and indignation that for a time every one was silent. Then followed varied expressions of horror, as each one realized that there existed a human being capable of committing an act so cruel, so full of unspeakable torment to its victims, as that of child stealing. The disguised writing, the evident effort at bad spelling, the absence of any signature, and the revelation of the fact that my child had been taken away for money, indicated that the wretch who designed the plot had carefully prepared to guard himself and his vile accomplices from detection. The officers were of the opinion that the abductors could not withhold or conceal the child many days. . . . With this oppressive weight on my mind, a sense of relief was felt on receiving the first information that Charley was alive, and that there was some hope that he would soon be safe at home. I was convinced that the writer of the letter had possession of Charley, not only because he declared it but more surely from the fact that he gave correctly Charley's middle name "Brewster," a name by which he was rarely called, but which was known to Walter, and was elicited from him during the drive to the city.

—CHRISTIAN ROSS, *THE FATHER'S STORY OF CHARLEY ROSS, THE KIDNAPPED CHILD*, 1876.

CHAPTER 13

Grave Matters

A. T. Stewart, 1878

In 1878, grave robbers broke into the crypt of department store magnate A. T. Stewart, stole his remains, and held them for ransom.

When department store magnate A. T. Stewart died in 1876, he left behind a fortune estimated at $40 million, but in 1878, grave robbers broke into his crypt, stole his remains, and held them for ransom. Neither his widow nor the executor refused to pay the ransom for the safe return of his remains.

AN HOUR BEFORE DAWN, ON THE MORNING OF NOVEMBER 7, 1878, THE assistant Sexton of Saint Mark's Church in the Bowery stumbled on a gruesome sight—a mound of freshly dug dirt lay at the opening to A. T. Stewart's family vault. Someone had broken into the tomb. Parker cried out and raced from the graveyard to inform the authorities. When the police arrived, they discovered that Stewart's coffin had been violated and his body removed. The ghouls had made their escape without leaving a single footprint to follow. The gruesome crime would convulse the city.

Shortly after the discovery of Stewart's grave robbery, letters began to pour into police department headquarters and to Henry Hilton, the executor of Stewart's will, and to Stewart's widow, Cornelia. The letters ranged from missives penned by spiritualists who claimed to have been in touch with the ghost of A. T. Stewart and knew the whereabouts of the missing remains to angry letters claiming that Stewart had gotten what he deserved. Finally, a letter sent from Canada claimed that the writer had Stewart's bones and was holding them for ransom in the amount of $200,000. The letter included a strip of purple velvet that was identified as coming from Stewart's coffin. Hilton refused to pay the ransom and instead hired Pinkerton detectives to investigate the case and offered a $25,000 reward for the apprehension and conviction of the culprits. Although initially inclined to pay the ransom, Cornelia changed her mind at Hilton's urging.

The grave robbery took precedent over every case in the city, and hundreds of police officers and detectives were assigned to the investigation. No stone was left unturned. Every lead, however absurd, was followed up on. A number of suspects were ultimately arrested but soon released when it was discovered that either publicity or heavy-handed police tactics had motivated their false confessions. The police watched all the ferries and railroad stations, stopping and questioning every suspicious looking character. Still, they were unable to uncover a single lead in the case.

At the time of his death from natural causes in April 1876, at the age of seventy-two, A. T. Stewart was the third wealthiest man in America, ranking behind only to William B. Astor Sr., who made his fortune in real estate, and Cornelius Vanderbilt, who became rich through railroad investments. Stewart left behind a fortune worth approximately $40 million to his wife, Cornelia. The executor of his will was Judge Henry Hilton, a close family friend and surrogate son to Stewart.

Stewart made his vast fortune in the retail sales business. He was known as "The Merchant Prince of Manhattan" and the father of the American department store. An Irish immigrant, he began his career in New York City in 1823 selling Irish linens. In 1846, he built the country's first department store on 280 Broadway, between Chambers and Reade Streets. The store was dubbed "The Marble Palace," because of its size and ornate marble façade. Inside were two ornamental columns representing the twin pillars of "Commerce and Plenty." There was a seventy-foot-wide rotunda with a balcony gallery overhead. High atop the building was a glass dome. Stewart planned his new store so that it included distinct departments, with a vast inventory for shoppers to choose from.

The Marble Palace sold imported European merchandise to women and provided fashion shows displaying the most recent styles and trends and in a lush ornate "Ladies Parlor" on the second floor where women lounged, talked, and refreshed themselves. The parlor was replete with full-length mirrors—another department store first initiated by Stewart.

In 1862, Stewart expanded his enterprises and built the largest department store in the world. Called the "The Iron Palace," Stewart's six-story store, located on the corner of Broadway and Ninth Street, had a cast iron front and a glass dome skylight. The structure took up a full city block and is thought to be the first building in New York City with a cast-iron front. The immense store employed over 2,000 people and had nearly twenty departments, selling everything from fabric to furniture.

Stewart later established department stores in different parts of the world, including London and Paris. Not only was Stewart the most successful retail sales tycoon in America, but he was also the first retailer to develop a successful mail-order business, earning an estimated annual income of $1 million a year from it. Stewart was the first to introduce the radical retail idea of one-price-for-all customers. Prior to this, shoppers often engaged in haggling with merchants about prices, trying to beat down the cost of various items. Merchants, in turn, would try to sell inferior goods at more than they were worth or misrepresent the products they were selling as new, when in fact they were inferior and outdated products. Stewart promised his customers that he would not sell anything in his store at a cost more than what its value was in the open market. He also vowed to his customers that if a particular product went down in its intrinsic worth, he would lower the price of the merchandise accordingly. So as not to portray Stewart as anything other than a shrewd businessman, at the same time, if the value of certain goods rose, he would increase the price accordingly.

He always bought his merchandise for cash, which gave him the advantage to buy goods and materials in large quantities at the best price. He was then able to sell his merchandise at a price that was fair, reasonable, and lower than market price. His formula for retail success was sound, simple, and successful. Soon most of the women in New York City became faithful and loyal customers.

In 1869, Stewart built an ornate home on the corner of Fifth Avenue and 34th Street in New York City. Unlike the other luxurious brownstone mansions located along what was referred to as "Millionaires Row," Stewart's was made entirely out of Italian marble cut exclusively for him in Italy and shipped to the United States. At a cost of approximately $2 million, it took seven years to build. Stewart's mansion had three main floors and an attic with a mansard roof. The elaborate home was separated from the sidewalks by a lighted moat and the main ballroom ran the full length of its Fifth Avenue frontage. Stewart filled the mansion with expensive furniture and antiques and a large and valuable art collection. His private art collection, including paintings, was estimated to be worth over $600,000.

His attempt to outdo his multimillionaire neighbors, like William and Caroline Astor, with the construction of his lavish home, did not endear him to New York City's powerful and affluent elite. Stewart and his wife found themselves ostracized by his wealthy neighbors, who viewed him as a millionaire upstart. He and his wife were snubbed for the most part by New York City's high society. Still, it did nothing to damage his retail empire. Although Stewart was not known as a philanthropist in league of Andrew Carnegie, he was still generous.

During the Irish potato famine of 1848, Stewart sent a shipload of provisions to his native Ireland and invited young people to take free passage to America where he found jobs for them within his vast department store complex. He also sent $50,000 to the victims of the Chicago fire. He built a "Woman's Hotel," in New York City, where working women could find safe, comfortable, and reasonably priced accommodations.

Stewart's most lasting philanthropic undertaking was the building of Garden City, New York. In 1869, he bought close to 7,000 acres on the Hempstead Plain on Long Island, where he built the first planned community in the United States for his workers. Garden City included sixteen miles of streets and avenues, a central park, affordable homes, stores, and a hotel. Stewart even built a railroad into the city so his workers could take the train to work at one of his many retail, wholesale, or manufacturing businesses. Stewart did not sell any of the property to the inhabitants but instead acted as landlord for the community, renting properties to workers. The Cathedral of the Incarnation, a massive, ornate edifice, was built in Garden City in 1885 by Cornelia Stewart at a cost of $2.5 million as a lasting memorial to her husband.

Finally, renowned detective, New York City police captain Thomas Byrnes claimed to have made a breakthrough in the sensational case when he arrested two men, Henry Vreeland and William Burke, charging them with the heinous crime. The two men led police on a merry chase through parts of New Jersey where they claimed the body was buried, until police discovered the men had concocted the whole story in the hopes of getting the reward. Vreeland and Burke were not prosecuted for the crime. Despite their dedication, the police remained stymied by the theft.

The gruesome crime captured the imagination of the American public and a media frenzy followed as newspapers tried to outdo each other in their sensational coverage. News of the theft of Stewart's remains was splashed across the headlines of every newspaper. The controversy swirled out of control in an ongoing flood of misinformation and wishful thinking, with each of the New York City newspapers periodically heralding a scoop on the case. As the investigation into Stewart's missing corpse dragged on with one clue after another leading nowhere, it proved to be an embarrassment to the police department. *Puck*, an irreverent New York City–based humor magazine, ran a series of unflattering cartoons and stories claiming the NYPD was simply incompetent. As if *Puck's* indictment wasn't enough, none other than America's premiere humorist, Mark Twain, got into the act, writing a parody of the police department's bungled investigation in 1879 called "The Stolen White Elephant."

Regardless of the ongoing investigation, no news regarding A. T. Stewart could have been more startling to the general public, aside from locating his remains and the culprits who stole them, than the front-page headlines that appeared in newspapers across the city on April 15, 1882. The once vast and profitable firm of A. T. Stewart & Co. was going out of business. Six years after Henry Hilton gained control of the company, the liquidation of the giant department store complex was announced. Hilton refused to accept blame for the company's demise and refused to acknowledge that the closing was predicated by a series of his business and public relations' blunders. Among those blunders included refusing accommodations to Jewish banker Joseph Seligman at The Grand Union in Saratoga and subsequently banning all members of the Jewish community from the resort hotel, which was owned and operated by the Stewart estate. Hilton's actions led to a boycott of Stewart's stores by New York City's Jewish community. Hilton also reneged on building the Working Woman's Hotel, claiming that as a charity for working women the hotel was a failure. Hilton announced that it would be remodeled and reopened as a commercial hotel operating under the name The Park Avenue Hotel. The abandonment of the Working Woman's hotel caused a furor among New York City women who also boycotted the department store.

Finally, in 1881, nearly five years after the ghoulish crime, Patrick Jones, a lawyer and former New York postmaster, contacted the widow of Stewart directly, reporting he had been in contact with the grave robbers and that they would return the bones for a $20,000 ransom. Without Henry Hilton's approval, Cornelia Stewart made arrangements, with Jones acting as an intermediary, for the return of her husband's remains. In late November 1881, on a cold, moonless night, on a deserted road in New York's Westchester County, two carriages crossed paths, one carriage driven by an emissary from Mrs. Stewart with the $20,000 ransom and the other driven by unidentified man.

The two carriages, each heading in opposite directions, stopped. One driver handed over a satchel with the $20,000 in exchange for a bag of bones. Ironically, the bag came from A. T. Stewart's department store. With the exchange made, the grave robbers raced off. The bones were taken by train to Garden City, where they were placed into the crypt at the Cathedral of the Incarnation. Positive identification of the bones was never made because Stewart's children predeceased him and there was no DNA testing at the time. The identity of the grave robbers was never discovered. Whether it is truly the bones of Alexander Turney Stewart buried at the Garden City Cathedral remains one of New York's enduring mysteries.

One mystery, however, does not remain. A. T. Stewart's fortune was squandered by Henry Hilton. He tried to replicate the vast success of his benefactor but all of his retail business endeavors were costly and abysmal failures. Despite this, Hilton did not curtail his lavish spending, buying splendid hotels and extravagant homes and bestowing himself and his family with luxuries, all at the expense of the dwindling Stewart fortune. Cornelia Stewart died on October 25, 1886, at the age of eighty-four years.

The Garden City community was ultimately sold and became the locale for many of Long Island's social set. The luxurious Stewart Marble Mansion remained vacant for a short period of time, and finally in 1890 it was rented to the New York City Manhattan Club, where it remained until 1899. In 1901, it was sold to a private corporation and was subsequently razed to make room for the Knickerbocker Trust Company, one of the largest banks in the country at the time. Stewart's original department store, the Marble Palace, was purchased by *The New York Sun* in 1917 where it remained until 1966. It is today primarily referred to as "The Sun Building." The building was declared a national landmark in 1965. Stewart's Cast Iron Palace was bought by John Wanamaker, a Philadelphia-based retail executive, in 1896, and he turned it into one of the leading department stores in New York City.

Wanamaker department store closed down its operations at that location in 1954, and in 1956, Stewart's Cast Iron burned down during a two-day fire. Henry Hilton died on August 24, 1899. He was seventy-five years old. A year before, much of the Stewart fortune was gone. Despite being the father of the American department store, nothing of A. T. Stewart's vast retail empire remains, his signature retail business gone forever from the American landscape and his name all but forgotten. Only his bones remain, tucked safely away in the crypt at the Cathedral of the Incarnation in Garden City, New York, and even they remain suspect.

The detectives say that on Thursday morning they found a blue-penciled letter "B" on one of the iron fence posts on the Second-avenue side and two posters bearing the name "Augustus Sebell" crossed on a post on the Eleventh-street side. These have since been removed, but the detectives say that by drawing imaginary lines from the two marked posts to two opposite trees the spot where the lines cross would be directly over the hole that was dug.
—THE NEW YORK TIMES, NOVEMBER 9, 1878.

Anything more depraved in the way of "journalism" than the behavior of the press during the past few days on the subject of the Stewart grave-robbery it would be difficult to conceive. The facts which have been published do not concern the public in any way. The thieves, having made away with the body, appear to have opened negotiations, as everybody knew they would do, with the Stewart family, through "counsel," and, the family having refused their terms, the matter was dropped. Is this any reason why we should now have column after column of the body-snatchers' letters, the replies of their "counsel" through the Herald "Personal" column, accompanied by details as to the condition of the corpse, followed by an acrimonious controversy as to whether Judge Hilton did or did not deceive Mrs. Stewart about the return of her husband's body, and persuade her that it had been returned while it had not? Some of the newspapers, while publishing all the details of the negotiations, dwell feelingly on the agony that the whole affair must have caused Mrs. Stewart, and the consequent heartless brutality of the thieves. What sort of work is this.
—THE NATION, JULY–DECEMBER, 1879.

CHAPTER 14

Easy Money

George Leslie, 1878

George Leslie, "King of Bank Robbers," was responsible for the largest bank robbery in America in 1878 when his gang robbed the Manhattan Savings Institution.

George Leslie, "King of Bank Robbers," was responsible for more than 80 percent of all the bank robberies in the country, and although his gang pulled off the largest bank robbery in American history in 1878, it was his roving eye, not his crimes, that led to his untimely demise.

On the morning of October 27, 1878, when bankers at the Manhattan Savings Institution, located at the corner of Bleecker Street and Broadway in New York City, opened their doors for business, to their horror, they discovered the bank had been broken into over the weekend and the bank vault emptied of cash and securities. It seemed impossible since the bank was known as one of the securest banks in the country. Still, it was true. Thieves had broken in and had stolen nearly $3 million. Based on current monetary standards, the Manhattan bank heist amounts to approximately $65 million, far surpassing any robbery ever in America, a record that still holds today. According to bank examiners, the exact amount the robbers stole was $2,747,700, nearly $2.5 million of which was in stocks and bonds. *The New York Times* hailed it as "the most sensational in the history of bank robberies in this country."

What made the robbery more incredible than just the amount was that the bank was one of the largest and most imposing in the world. The Manhattan Savings Institution was not just a bank, but it was also a depository for the money, jewelry, securities, and other valuables of some of the most prominent and wealthy citizens of New York City, among them Andrew Carnegie, John D. Rockefeller, Jay Gould, James Fisk Jr., and Cornelius Vanderbilt. It was a ponderous labyrinth of bolts, locks, and steel doors, making it an almost impregnable fortress.

It took criminal mastermind George Leslie three years to plan the robbery down to the minutest detail. Leslie, a dashing, handsome, University of Cincinnati–educated architect, who came to New York City in 1869, was dubbed "The King of Bank Robbers" by New York City police, newspaper reporters, and underworld figures. According to law enforcement authorities, from 1869 to 1878 Leslie was responsible for more than 80 percent of all the bank robberies in the country, either by planning the robberies or by carrying them out himself. Despite his reputation, Leslie was never apprehended and never spent a day of his life in jail.

Leslie was responsible for the three biggest bank heists in history. Besides the Manhattan bank job, he was responsible for the 1869 Ocean National Bank robbery in New York City that netted thieves $800,000, then considered the largest robbery of the era, and the 1876 Northampton Bank robbery in Massachusetts, where a record-breaking $1.6 million in cash and securities were stolen. Not a shot was fired in any of his robberies. Not a single person was injured. Not a stick of dynamite was used. And not one bit of property was destroyed. Nothing like it had ever been pulled off in the annals of New York City crime. It was all done with Leslie's characteristic finesse. Even the city newspapers gave credit to the culprits: "A masterful bank job pulled off by one very special bank robber," *The New York Herald* reported after the Manhattan robbery.

All of Leslie's bank jobs were arduous undertakings. He would meticulously survey the bank's layout and then, using his training and talent as an architect, he would draw blueprints of the bank. Inside an abandoned warehouse, he would build a replica of the bank vault, where he would rehearse the robbery with his handpicked gang for months. No one had ever gone to the extent Leslie did in planning a bank robbery. At the vacant warehouse, Leslie rehearsed with his gang how the entire operation would work, with each member of the gang performing a specific function at a specific time. He had all the gang study the blueprints and drilled into them the step-by-step process they would take during the robbery.

Leslie timed each of the steps so that everything would be done with split-second precision. Timing was everything as far as Leslie was concerned. Leslie also repeatedly reenacted the bank heist, throwing in various possibilities and forecasting alternative measures. He even had the gang reenact the robbery in the dark in case something happened to the lighting inside the bank. Leslie always planned to have his robberies on the weekends when the banks were closed for business. Then bank officials and authorities would not discover the robbery until the following Monday morning, giving Leslie and his gang plenty of time to rob the bank and make their getaways.

Prior to his emergence into the crime world, bank burglars used dynamite to blow open a bank vault. The robbers often blew up more than just the door. Hundreds of times robbers used too much dynamite and ended up blowing up all the cash, securities, and other valuables inside— or, worse, blowing themselves up. And the blast from using dynamite drew attention and caused panic, which led to many failed robbery attempts.

Besides being able to draw blueprints of the banks and his obsession with rehearsing the robberies, Leslie brought another bank robbing tool to the table—"the little joker." Although he did not invent it, the credit for that goes to another New York City criminal, Max Shinburn. Leslie perfected its use. The "little joker" was a small tin wheel with a wire attached to it, which would fit inside the combination knob of any bank safe. All anyone had to do was take off the dial knob of a bank safe and place the little joker on the inside of the dial. Then, after carefully replacing the knob, it could be left there undetected. When bank officials opened the safe the next day during regular business hours, "the little joker," still concealed under the safe's knob, would record where the tumblers stopped by making a series of deep cuts in the tin wheel. The deepest cuts in the wheel showed the numbers of the combination. Although it wouldn't record the exact order of the numbers in the combination, it would only be a matter of trying several different combinations before the safe would open. A bank robber could sneak back into the bank, remove the knob, examine the marks in the tin plate, and figure out the exact order in which the stops were used.

Using the device *did* require a robber to break into a bank twice— once to place the contraption inside the dial of the vault and a second time to retrieve it. Not many robbers had the aptitude or patience to perform such a tricky endeavor. It took a special, meticulous kind of person to accomplish the undertaking, someone with brains, patience, and nerves of steel. George Leslie was that person. Although time-consuming, "the little joker" eliminated the need to use dynamite to blow open a safe and the need for the usual long or the laborious safecracking techniques used by many robbers—of turning the dial this way and that, listening with a stethoscope to determine the right sequence of combination clicks. Leslie sometimes broke into a bank two or three times in order to place and retrieve his "little joker" without ever once being caught. He was able to do this by bribing the bank's night watchman to let him into the bank, or, on several occasions, after depositing a considerable sum of his own money in the targeted bank and becoming a valued customer, he was able to convince the bank to hire one of his cronies as a watchman.

Twenty-seven-year-old George Leslie arrived in New York City in 1869, the son of a prosperous Cincinnati brewer, a graduate of the University of Cincinnati, and a successful architect. With his good looks, education, and fine manners, he ingratiated himself into New York City's high society, became a patron of the arts, attended the opera, and was invited to only the best New York City parties. But Leslie led a double life. Despite being able to slip seamlessly through the many layers of New York City's high society, no one ever suspected he was the same man known as "The King of Bank Robbers."

Before leaving Cincinnati, Leslie told friends he wanted to make some "easy money" in New York City. Leslie had no intention of resuming his architectural career and had no interest becoming a Wall Street investor, although he had a small family fortune to play with. Coming to New York City, leaving behind old friends and family (his mother and father had both died, and he had no siblings), shedding the baggage of his past, Leslie set his sights on a life of crime. He intended to make his "easy money" by becoming a bank robber—but not just any old run-of-the-mill bank robber but the best, the most successful, and the richest.

If ever there was a place to begin a criminal career, New York City was it. A would-be bank robber like Leslie couldn't have been better situated. The wealthiest men and women in the country made New York City their home, which meant they kept their money, jewels, stocks, and other valuables in banks and there seemed to be a bank on every corner of the city. There had to be millions of dollars just sitting there, waiting for the right kind of bank robber to come along and make an unlawful withdrawal. George Leslie intended to be that robber.

It was the Civil War that drove Leslie from his Cincinnati home to the bustling metropolis of New York City. The bloodiest conflict in the country's history had come to an end just four years prior to his arrival in the city, and the wounds were still fresh for both North and South. Close to 3.5 million men fought in the war, and nearly 700,000, both Union and Confederate, troops died. A million more were maimed or wounded.

Although George Leslie wasn't one of them, it wasn't luck that had saved him, it was money—his father's money.

Men and women, fathers and sons, brothers and sisters, women and children—all suffered through the four bloodiest years in American history. Leslie's home state, Ohio, provided a quarter million able-bodied men as soldiers and military officers during the war. Thousands of young men from Cincinnati flocked to Union military service at the outset of the war in 1861 or were drafted, but Leslie wasn't one of them. There was a provision in the Union Conscription Act of 1863 that allowed wealthy men to pay $300 to buy their way out of service. Leslie's father paid the money, allowing Leslie to avoid serving. Although it was perfectly legal, it became a highly unpopular course of action, and one that many did not forget after the war ended. Wealthy young men like George Leslie could not have been thought less of. They were considered worse than deserters. After the war was over, Leslie found himself in the position of facing public scorn from many in Cincinnati. There was open hostility toward him, and he was ostracized by many Cincinnati families and former friends who had served or lost someone in battle. Their resentment overwhelmed him. He wanted to start over in some place new where no one knew him or about the albatross that hung around his neck from his conduct during the war. New York City was the perfect place to lose and then reinvent himself.

Leslie intended the Manhattan robbery to be the final jewel in his crown as "King of the Bank Robbers." He would have enough money from the robbery to quit the bank robbery business, move out to the West, and once again reinvent himself. He sent his wife to Philadelphia to hide. All the plans were in place. If Leslie had another flaw in his character, it was his attraction to women. Known as a ladies' man, he engaged in a slew of romantic liaisons with women from both sides of the tracks— high society and criminals. He wasn't particularly discerning nor was he discriminating when it came to single or married women and this led to his downfall.

In May 1878, five months before Leslie planned to rob the Manhattan Savings Institution, he stopped at Murphy's Saloon in Brooklyn. Someone in the saloon approached him and handed him a note. He recognized the handwriting. It was from Babe Draper, the twenty-one-year-old wife of one of his gang members, Shang Draper. Draper was an infamous criminal and thug. Leslie had been secretly carrying on an affair with Shang's wife Babe. In the note, Babe asked to see Leslie one last time before the bank robbery and his flight from New York City forever. Leslie couldn't resist. He left the bar to have his last secret rendezvous with Babe.

On June 4, 1878, George Leslie's body was discovered at the foot of Tramp's Rock, in Mott's Woods, three miles from Yonkers. His body was partly decomposed and lying under some bushes. He had been shot twice, once in the heart and once in the head. Leslie was just forty years old. The murder of George Leslie was never officially solved, although police investigators surmised that Leslie had been lured to his death by Babe Draper and killed by her husband, who had found out about the illicit affair. The King of Bank Robbers, the man responsible for robbing or masterminding the robbery of millions of dollars, was buried in a $10 pauper's grave in the Cypress Hill Cemetery. Not long after Leslie's body was discovered, Babe Draper's body was found in the waters near the Brooklyn Bridge, her throat slit.

On October 27, 1878, five months after Leslie's murder, his gang, including Shang Draper, broke in and robbed the Manhattan Savings Institution. One of the largest investigations in New York City police annals began immediately following the heist, and slowly, one by one, the men who robbed the Manhattan Savings Institution were tracked down and brought to justice—all except George Leslie. Leslie, the architect from Cincinnati, who had been looking to make some "easy money," had pulled off the biggest bank heist in history, but he never lived to see it. Easy money was harder to come by than he thought.

The robbery was almost the sole topic of conversation in financial circles to-day. Early this morning crowds of people assembled in the vicinity of the bank building at Broadway and Bleecker Street. In the throng were many depositors who had come thereto ascertain what possibility there was of getting their money. . . . The Manhattan Savings Institution was on the morning of Sunday, October 27, robbed *of securities to the amount of $2,747,700, of which $2,506,700 are registered and not negotiable. . . . Werckle was at the bank to-day. He is a small, sickly looking German with weak features and a manner that denotes indecision. He told the story of the robbery substantially as it has been published. The combination of the door of the outer vault which he gave the thieves and by which they opened it was 80–9–25. The combination was changed to-day. . . . Mr. Alvord, Secretary of the Bank, assured an EAGLE reporter to-day that the loss in any event would not exceed $85,000, and it would, in all probability, fall below that figure. Some inconvenience would be caused by the loss of the bonds, but they would either be speedily recovered or a new issue would be made . . . the work of the burglars, indicate their expressed opinion that the case is without its rival in the annals of the force, and that the whole sagacity and shrewdness of the force will necessarily be called into play to effect the capture of the burglars. Pinkerton detectives have received instructions to go to work on the case and they are now very busy.*

—*Brooklyn Daily Eagle*, October 29, 1878.

The funeral of George Howard [Leslie], the burglar, who was found murdered in Mott's Woods, on Palmer-avenue, Yonkers, took place at noon yesterday from the establishment of J. J. Diehl, undertaker. . . . . The publication of the fact that the funeral would take place from Diehl's drew a large crowd of curious spectators to the neighborhood. Detective King said last night that he had not succeeded in discovering the whereabouts of the woman "Lizzie," the mistress of Howard, but had obtained information which he declined to make public, but which he said would lead to her discovery within the next 24 hours, if not sooner. . . . Howard's [Leslie's] wife in Philadelphia has telegraphed that she is destitute of means to pay her fare to this City. Notwithstanding this excuse, however, and in spite of the assertion made by the undertaker Diehl, that there were no women at the funeral of Leslie, it was learned late last night, positively, that Howard's [Leslie's] widow was there. . . . An elderly woman and two young women were also present. These with four young men were the only persons who were permitted to enter the undertaker's shop. The elderly woman is well known to the Police, but her name is withheld by them. She was visibly affected while looking upon the features of the dead burglar. . . . Two of the young men were professional thieves, another was a respectable man who had known [Howard] Leslie while alive, but was ignorant of his true character, and the fourth was a casual acquaintance. . . . Mrs. Howard [Leslie] and her brother, and a number of others who had waited outside, followed the remains to the grave.

—*THE NEW YORK TIMES,* JUNE 10, 1878.

CHAPTER 15

Good Fences Make Good Neighbors

Fredericka Mandelbaum, 1884

Fredericka Mandelbaum, a Jewish immigrant, came to America in 1850 where she became the leader of one of America's first crime syndicates and accumulated more money and power than any woman of her era engaged in legitimate business.

Fredericka "Marm" Mandelbaum, a German Jewish immigrant, came to America in 1850 where she became the most influential crime figure in New York City during the Gilded Age, accumulating more money and power than any woman of her era at a level inconceivable for any women engaged in legitimate business.

On July 22, 1884, with an arrest warrant in hand, undercover Pinkerton detective Gustav Frank approached the carriage in front of Fredericka Mandelbaum's haberdashery shop. Inside the carriage were Mandelbaum, her twenty-four-year-old son Julius, and her most trusted confidant Herman Stoude. Detective Frank had spent five months working undercover to catch Mandelbaum receiving stolen merchandise. Stepping into the carriage, flanked by a cadre of Pinkerton detectives, Frank waved the arrest warrant in her face and triumphantly proclaimed, "You are caught this time, and the best thing that you can do is to make a clean breast of it." Mandelbaum responded by punching Frank in the nose and knocking him from the carriage. "So, you are the one who is at the bottom of this, you wretch you!" she snapped. The other detectives had to restrain her from striking him again.

Mandelbaum and the others in the carriage were arrested and transported to the Harlem Police Court for arraignment. She was released on $30,000 bail. Even with several judges on her payroll, Mandelbaum was not able to squirm out of the charges. The New York district attorney saw to it that Mandelbaum's case would be heard by an incorruptible judge. It became clear to Mandelbaum that despite all the legal wrangling by her lawyers and the calling in of every political favor she was owed, nothing could be done to stop the case from going to court in December. According to her attorneys, it looked like she would be found guilty, after decades of eluding prosecution.

Between the time of her arrest and the pending trial in early December, Pinkerton detectives were on around-the-clock surveillance of Mandelbaum's home, keeping tabs on her every move. On the day before the trial, Mandelbaum came out of her house dressed all in black, the feather plumes on her small hat bobbing in front of her face. She waved to the detectives, who by now acknowledged their cover had been blown. She climbed into her carriage and went to her lawyers' office. The detectives followed close behind. She exited the carriage and went inside. She had made several trips to visit her lawyers during the time she was out on bail, and there was nothing unusual about it. She stayed for a time, came back out, waved again at the detectives, climbed back into the carriage, and was driven home. The detectives followed.

But it wasn't Mandelbaum who had exited her lawyers' office. It was a maid, who worked for Mandelbaum, who climbed into the carriage and sped off with the detectives in hot pursuit. The maid was approximately the same height and weight as Mandelbaum and was dressed exactly like her, including the tiny hat with the plumes covering her face and true identity. After it was determined that the coast was clear, the real Mandelbaum exited the law offices, boarded a waiting carriage, and made a clean getaway to Canada.

Mandelbaum began her climb to the top of the crime world as a peddler on the rough-and-tumble, bustling streets of New York City. Because of her height (she was close to six feet tall) and her massive girth (she weighed close to 300 pounds), she easily stood out among the throng of street vendors. But it was more than just her physical presence that drew people to her. She quickly established a reputation as a fair trader among legitimate customers as well as a trusted ally to criminals trying to sell their stolen goods. It was this latter quality that led her to become the most sought-after fence (a receiver and seller of stolen property) in New York City and propelled her to a place of prominence in the criminal world. She was a driving force behind New York City's festering underworld for more than twenty-five years. A July 1884 *The New York Times* article called her "the nucleus and center of the whole organization of crime in New York City."

Mandelbaum was savvy enough to realize, even in the earliest years of her climb to power, that she could not carry on her business without the support of the city's corrupt political powers, the judicial system, and the police—from the cop on the beat to those in command. Knowing full well the power of the almighty dollar and how it fed the ongoing corruption at every level, she paid bribes to these forces of politicians, police, and judges religiously, which allowed her criminal operation to grow and thrive unabated throughout the years.

By 1864, her enterprise, buying stolen merchandise from criminals and reselling it at a profit, had become so successful that she was able to move off the streets and buy a three-story building at Clinton and Rivington Streets, where she opened a haberdashery shop on the ground floor. For decades, it served as a respectable front for the biggest fencing operation in the history of the country.

Mandelbaum kept the prestigious law firm of Howe & Hummel, two of the most devious and successful criminal lawyers in country, on a $5,000-a-year retainer. Whenever one of her gang got into trouble, she offered her criminal cohorts bail and legal defense if they needed it and bribed police and judges to fix cases. She ran a well-organized criminal enterprise, enlisting the services of an extensive network of criminals. She called her cadre of criminals her "little chicks." They called her "Marm" which was short for "mother," because like a mother hen, she hovered over them, guiding and nurturing their notorious careers. "They call me Ma because I give them money and horses and diamonds," she reportedly said.

She was also partial to helping young women get a foothold in the criminal world. She was once quoted as saying that she wanted to help any women who "are not wasting life being a housekeeper." Because of her efforts to help women find work, even if it was in the world of crime, some contemporary feminist historians view Mandelbaum as a Gilded Age heroine for her willingness to assist women find work and helping them make more money than they could have as housekeepers, maids, seamstresses, or factory workers.

By 1880, she had become the premier receiver of stolen merchandise in the country and one of the most powerful figures within organized crime, amassing a personal fortune estimated at more than $1 million. She owned tenements in the city as well as warehouses in New Jersey and Brooklyn where she stored stolen merchandise that she openly bought and sold. As her business flourished, she was able to furnish the living quarters on the second floor of her business with expensive furniture, draperies, paintings, and silverware that had been stolen from some of the finest homes and mansions in New York City.

Mandelbaum was begrudgingly accepted into polite society, despite everyone's wide knowledge of her criminal enterprise. She held ostentatious dinner parties at her home, where many of the country's most celebrated criminals mingled freely with countless members of New York City's fashionable elite, including judges, police, legitimate businessmen, and politicians, including two of the most corrupt and powerful politicians of the era: Mayor Fernando Woods, considered the most corrupt mayor in the city's history, and William Marcy "Boss" Tweed, the prototypical corrupt political boss. Everyone who was anyone cherished the opportunity to be invited to one of her many soirées.

Mandelbaum once arranged a successful jailbreak to get her favorite piano player, the notorious safecracker Piano Charley Bullard, out of prison since she missed the piano concertos he gave at her extravagant parties. Bullard, a handsome, raffish, classically educated, piano-playing safecracker, who squandered his ill-gotten gains on wine, women, and gambling, was one of Mandelbaum's favorite "little chicks." After robbing $450,000 from the Boylston Bank in Boston, Bullard fled to London and later moved to Paris, where he opened a popular expatriate bar called "The American Bar." He died in a Belgium prison in 1892.

Mandelbaum opened a school for crime on Grand Street, where young boys and girls were taught the intricacies of the criminal trade by professional pickpockets, burglars, and sneak thieves. The school offered advanced courses in burglary, safecracking, blackmailing, and confidence schemes. She allegedly had to close the school when it was discovered that the son of one of the city's most prominent police officials was enrolled in it.

One of the school's most infamous students and one of Mandelbaum's protégés, Sophie Lyons, became one of America's most successful confidence women, known appropriately enough, because of her close tutelage by Mandelbaum, as "The Princess of Crime." Mandelbaum saw in the young and beautiful Lyons the image of how she wished she had been. Mandelbaum, tall, fat, and unattractive, was drawn to the waif-like beauty of Lyons. Since Mandelbaum forbid her own daughters from engaging in any criminal activity, she desired to have someone, a woman in particular, learn the ropes from her. Lyons was her choice. Beautiful, smart, and daring, Lyons became was one of the country's most notorious criminals. Despite her long and close relationship with Mandelbaum, in her book *Why Crime Does Not Pay*, published in 1913, Lyons turned against her benefactor and mentor, portraying Mandelbaum as a criminal predator, someone who had coerced and seduced her into a life of crime.

Mandelbaum financed one of the greatest bank robberies in America by fronting the operations of George Leslie and his gang of burglars. Leslie was known as "The King of Bank Robbers," a title given to him by criminal associates, as well as police and newspapers. A criminal mastermind, Leslie was credited by police for being responsible for, one way or another, either by planning or by personally carrying out, 80 percent of the bank robberies in the country during the early part of America's Gilded Age. In October 1878, his gang broke into the Manhattan Savings Institution and stole close to $3 million in cash and securities, comparable to approximately $75 million in today's currency.

Mandelbaum's reign as "Queen of Thieves" came to an end in 1884 when New York City's avowed crime-fighting district attorney, Peter Olney, with the help of Pinkerton detectives, caught Mandelbaum in a sting operation. Undercover detective Gustav Frank sold Mandelbaum several bolts of stolen silk that had been secretly marked. When detectives raided her store and found the stolen silk in her possession, they arrested her.

Out on bail, while awaiting trial, and, although under constant surveillance by Pinkerton detectives, she eluded authorities and jumped bail fleeing to Canada, with more than $1 million in cash and diamonds. She settled in Hamilton, Ontario. Canada had no extradition agreement with America at the time, so she was able to live out the rest of her life comfortably, snubbing her nose at the long arm of the American law.

In November 1885, the sudden death of her eighteen-year-old daughter, Annie, brought her back to New York City. Mandelbaum slipped into the city to pay her last respects. It was widely reported that she was in the city despite the indictments that were still hanging over her head. Whether or not District Attorney Olney, Pinkerton detectives, or the police took pity on Mandelbaum's situation is unknown, but what is known is that she put her daughter to rest in a public ceremony and was unhampered by the police. She returned to her Canadian home following the funeral.

During the ensuing years, whether because of her daughter's sudden death, or homesickness for her old New York neighborhood or just plain old age, Mandelbaum was besieged by a series of illnesses. She died on February 26, 1894, at the age of sixty-five. Although the obituary notice that appeared in the *Hamilton Spectator* took note of her criminal past, it called her "a woman of kindly disposition, broad sympathies, and large intelligence." Her body was returned to New York City for burial at the family plot in Union Fields Cemetery of Congregation Rodeph Sholom in Queens. A huge crowd of mourners, including old friends and neighbors, businessmen, police officials, politicians, judges, newspaper reporters, curiosity seekers, and a score of well-known criminals, all turned out to pay their last respects to the "Queen of Thieves." Ironically, following Mandelbaum's graveside service, several dozen mourners reported to police that their pockets had been picked.

It would take a woman of great determination and entrepreneurial skill to move from subsistence peddling to great wealth and power. She scrutinized the workings of the economic landscape and used what she had and saw to make a living and increase her income and power.
—FREDERICKA RONA HOLUB, *"MARM" MANDELBAUM,*
"QUEEN OF THE FENCES": THE RISE AND FALL OF
A FEMALE IMMIGRANT CRIMINAL ENTREPRENEUR IN
NINETEENTH-CENTURY NEW YORK CITY, 2007.

She was shrewd, careful and methodical in character and to the point in speech. Wary in the extreme she never admitted anyone unknown to her or unvouched for beyond the precincts of the little dry goods store.
—GEORGE WASHINGTON WALLING, *RECOLLECTIONS*
OF A NEW YORK CHIEF OF POLICE, 1887.

The peculiarity and the disgrace of this case is that in New York only has the receiving and sale of stolen goods been carried on for many years as openly as if it were a legitimate industry. Mrs. MANDEL-BAUM'S business has been as much under the protection of the law as the business of any one of the firms whose stolen goods constituted her stock in trade. The woman's character has been known during all these years to every detective and to every police magistrate in New

York . . . her intimacy with the detectives of the police force was only less close and confidential than her intimacy with the thieves. . . . The prosperous career for twenty years of the woman MANDELBAUM as a notorious receiver of stolen goods has itself been an indictment of the police force.

—THE NEW YORK TIMES, JULY 24, 1884.

CHAPTER 16

Jolly Jane

Jane Toppan, 1889

Nurse Jane Toppan, known as "Jolly Jane," was one of the most prolific serial killers in American history, poisoning a reported 32 people.

Nurse Jane Toppan, known as "Jolly Jane," because of her bubbly personality, was one of the most prolific serial killers in American history, poisoning thirty-one people she knew or was charged with caring for during a fifteen-year murder spree.

IN FEBRUARY 1900, TOPPAN POISONED HER OLD FRIEND, MYRA CONNERS, with strychnine, in order to take over her position as dining matron at the Theological School. After Myra died, Toppan went to the dean of the Theological School and informed him that Conners was planning on going on a sabbatical and she had intended to recommend her for the job. She lied to the dean and told him that Conners had instructed her on all of the duties of the job.

The dean offered Jane the job and, right from the start, her coworkers questioned her competence. During the summer, while the Theological School was out of session, she worked at the mess hall of the Biological School in Woods Hole. In November 1900, she was dismissed from her job at the Theological School for financial irregularities and complaints that had been lodged against her. Luckily, she claimed no victims there.

She was known as "Jolly Jane," to her friends and associates because of her ability to energize any occasion with jokes and family stories. She was a stout Irish spinster with rosy red cheeks and sparkling dark eyes. She was born in 1857 as Honora Kelley and was raised in the Boston Female Asylum, an orphanage on Washington Street in the South End. Her parents were Irish immigrants. Her mother died of tuberculosis when she was very young and her father, Peter Kelley, was an abusive, eccentric alcoholic. He was given the nickname "Kelley the Crack," referring to crackpot. An example of his bizarre behavior is that he once sewed his eyelids shut while working as a tailor.

In 1863, only a few years after his wife's death, he took his two youngest children, eight-year-old Delia and six-year-old Honora, to the Boston Female Asylum, an orphanage for indigent female children.

In November 1864, Honora Kelley was placed as an indentured servant in the home of Mrs. Ann Toppan of Lowell, Massachusetts. Though never formally adopted by the Toppans, Honora took the surname of her patrons and ultimately became known as Jane.

While she seemed "jolly" and content on the outside, on the inside she boiled against her privileged foster sister, Elizabeth Toppan, who acquired the family fortune along with a marriage to an upstanding deacon, Oramel Brigham. Elizabeth Toppan was beautiful, genteel, and well liked, everything Jane was not. They did not get along. Some say the hatred they had for each other is what made Jane become so bitter. While Elizabeth inherited the Toppan family fortune and married, Jane was jilted by a suitor who called off an engagement. After that, her resentment of Elizabeth Brigham turned to hatred.

In 1885, she began working as a nurse, training at Cambridge Hospital on Mount Auburn Street. Working on the various wards at night, she began to conduct what she later called "scientific experiments" on patients. Her favorite tools were morphine, which caused the pupils to contract and breathing to slow down, ultimately leading to coma. This was followed by using atropine on the same patient, a drug derived from the belladonna plant that has the opposite effect.

By mixing the two drugs, she consecutively descended her victims into inertness, and then revived them to elevations of delirium, until she administered a final dose to kill them. Accordingly, while engaged in this horrific condition, she whipped herself into a sexual frenzy. A patient who survived her poisoning attempt described how Toppan climbed into bed with her and pressed against her, stroking her hair and caressing her through her bedclothes.

She soon moved on to Mass General, where she continued her experiments on patients. After too many of her patients died, she was summarily dismissed from the hospital by administrators who simply thought her careless with her dosages and did not conduct autopsies. Beginning in 1891, she went to work as a private nurse to some of the most distinguished families in the cities of Boston and Cambridge.

Soon she began escalating her list of victims well beyond unsuspecting hospital patients. She poisoned her landlords to avoid paying rent. She killed a friend in hopes of getting her job at a seminary.

In 1895, she killed her landlord, Israel Dunham. Two years later, she poisoned his wife, Lovey, with whom she lived. Later that year, she poisoned Mary McLear, aged seventy years, after she was recommended by the woman's doctor to take care of her. It was speculated that Toppan took some of McLear's clothing. This murder was odd because Toppan did not know Mary personally, and she generally liked to kill people that she knew.

In 1899, she walked with her foster sister, Elizabeth Brigham, down to the beach on Buzzards Bay for a picnic. Toppan fed her poison. Elizabeth was unable to get out of bed the next day, and, two days later, she died.

The doctor who examined Elizabeth proclaimed the sudden death was from a "stroke of apoplexy." Elizabeth Brigham's distressed husband thanked Toppan for caring so tenderly for his wife in her last moments. In her confession, years later, Toppan said her half-sister Elizabeth was "really the first of my victims that I actually hated and poisoned with vindictive purpose."

"I held her in my arms and watched with delight as she gasped her life out," Jane later said.

In 1901, Toppan began with new landlords, Melvin and Eliza Beedle, in Cambridge, Massachusetts. She poisoned them but only enough to give them gastrointestinal illness. Toppan then poisoned the Beedles' housekeeper, Mary Sullivan, enough to frame her as drunk so she would be dismissed and Toppan could take over her job. After that, Toppan became even more bold, poisoning the entire Davis family who were the owners of the cottage where she lived in Buzzards Bay in 1901.

In June of that year, the landlord of the cottage where Jane vacationed decided that it was time to collect on the $500 she owed them. Mary Davis went to the Beedles' house in Cambridge where Toppan gave her morphine mixed in her drinking water. Alden became sick and, over the next seven days, lapsed into a coma and died. Toppan then moved in with the Davis family to help take care of the grieving husband, Alden Davis. Less than a week after she had been there, Jane set fire to some papers in a closet in her new home. Much to Jane's dismay, the fire was quickly extinguished. A few days later, Jane lit a fire in the pantry and went out for an afternoon stroll. Fortunately for the Davis family, friends saw the smoke and rushed to put the fire out. The next week, Jane set another fire in the Davis home, but once again, it was extinguished in time.

In July, she poisoned Genevieve Gordon, the youngest of the Davis daughters, who had remained in the house to take care of her father. Toppan tried to pass Gordon's murder as a suicide, claiming Gordon was distraught over her mother's death.

In August, Toppan decided to murder Alden Davis. She killed him less than two weeks after his youngest daughter's death. In mid-August 1901, Toppan poisoned the last of the Davis family—the oldest daughter, Minnie Gibbs. While Minnie was dying, Jane brought her ten-year-old son to bed with her.

In late August of that year, Toppan returned to her hometown of Lowell, in hopes of marrying her dead foster-sister's widower, Deacon Oramel Brigham. Toppan killed his sister, Edna Bannister, aged seventy-seven, because she felt she was in the way of her marriage to Brigham.

Although Jolly Jane had managed to get away with the murders for years, the coincidences around these deaths were too great to ignore. Toppan returned to Cambridge, where she poisoned Oramel Brigham's seventy-year-old sister, Edna Barrister, whom she felt was an obstacle to her marriage to him. She even poisoned Oramel, so she could prove her love and worth to him by nursing him back to health. She even poisoned herself to evoke his sympathy. It didn't work. Brigham demanded she leave his house.

In the meantime, authorities on Cape Cod were exhuming the Davis family's bodies suspecting that they had been poisoned. They arrested Toppan that fall, and tied her to the murder weapon when a local pharmacist told them he'd sold Toppan enough morphine to send into eternal rest "a score of persons." On August 31, 1901, Minnie Gibbs's father-in-law, Captain Gibbs, summoned Leonard Wood—the leading toxicologist in Massachusetts—to exhume the bodies of the Davis family to test his suspicions that they had been poisoned. Jane read this in the newspaper. When the bodies were exhumed, a state police detective, John S. Patterson, was assigned to follow Jane and keep an eye on her.

Toppan went to New Hampshire to visit an old friend, Sarah Nichols, and, in late October 1901, she was arrested for the murder of Minnie Gibbs and returned to Massachusetts. During the entire time that Jane was awaiting a formal trial, she remained in the Barnstable Jailhouse. She quickly befriended the jailor's wife, who believed that Jane was innocent. As she sat in her jail cell, Jane gained more and more weight. The arraignment was held for her on October 31. The trial continued until November 8. Toppan pled not guilty.

The state proposed that Jane had been using arsenic to poison her victims because it had been found in the bodies. It turned out that the embalming fluid used was mostly arsenic and the prosecution was at a standstill about how Jane had killed her victims. It was Captain Gibbs, Minnie Gibbs's father-in-law, who purposed that Jane had used morphine and atropine as her poisons of choice.

The trial was adjourned to November 11. An inquisition hearing about the deaths of the Davis girls was held after Toppan's hearing, and Captain Gibbs's suspicions were proved correct. Toppan's trial continued until December 11. Toppan was officially charged with four counts of murder of the entire Davis family. Once again, she pled not guilty.

The newspapers reported that Toppan had undergone a psychiatric evaluation by a panel of experts who had determined that she was insane. She had admitted that she had an irresistible sexual impulse to kill and she confessed to eleven murders. It took less than eight hours for the entire trial, and the jury only had to deliberate for twenty minutes. Toppan was found not guilty by reason of insanity. She was sentenced to the Taunton Insane Hospital for life.

In her last confession, printed in the *New York Journal*, she boasted about fooling doctors for years, and regretted only that she tipped her hand by poisoning "four people in one family almost at once. That was the greatest mistake of my life."

"If all of the suspicions involving the operations of Jane Toppan could be substantiated in the opinion of men acquainted with the investigations in Cataumet, Cambridge and Lowell, the succession of murders will cover a wider range and be more astounding than any series of crimes perpetuated by one person in many years," claimed an article in the November 1, 1901, edition of *The Sun*.

Toppan blamed her crimes on the fiancé who jilted her decades before. She wrote: "I still laughed and was jolly, but I learned how to hate, too. If I had been a married woman, I probably would not have killed all these people."

Soon after the trial, the *New York Journal* published what it reported was Toppan's confession to her lawyer claiming that she had killed more than thirty-one people and that she wanted the jury to find her insane so she could eventually have a chance at being released.

Toppan was overcome with joy about the verdict because she assumed that she would be able to convince the hospital of her sanity and be set free in a few months' time. It was later discovered that Toppan had confessed to her defense lawyer, James Stuart Murphy, that she had committed more than thirty-one murders. In addition to this, as a supplement to the *New York Journal*, William Randolph Hearst typed up Jane's confession. In this document, Toppan admitted that she wanted the panel of psychiatrists to find her insane. After convincing them of her lie, she felt very smug in knowing that she had outsmarted a panel of "experts." She described the exquisite pleasure it gave her to kill her patients, and she marveled at the lack of feeling and remorse she felt for doing these horrible things. In an attempt to show that she was not without feeling, Jane claimed that the jilt she received from the lover in her youth seemed to be the root cause of all of her problems. Jane explained, "If I had been a married woman, I probably would not have killed all of those people. I would have had my husband, my children and my home to take up my mind."

Toppan lived out the rest of her days in the Taunton Lunatic Asylum—becoming increasingly deranged and paranoid as the years went on. In letters to lawyers and doctors, she repeatedly accused hospital staff of trying to poison her. She died in 1938 at the age of eighty-one confined to the Taunton State Hospital.

JANE TOPPAN, the poisoner of thirty-one persons, after two and a half years' confinement in the Insane hospital here, is approaching—has reached—the secondary stage of her ailment, moral insanity, and is believed to be near her end, says a Taunton, Mass., correspondent of the New York Times. Until within a short period the visitor to the hospital was unable to observe even the least trace of insanity. The question used to be asked, "Why is she here? She seems as sane as her attendants." But now her mental delusions are frequent, almost constant, and were anyone outside to see her there would be no doubt of the appropriateness of her incarceration. She has abandoned the careless, cheerful frame of mind in which she has heretofore been and is now fretful, peevish, even ugly, fault-finding, fearful of eating because of suspected poison, complaining of her treatment, morose—everything but remorseful. The intellectual insanity, following the moral Insanity with which it is now believed Jane Toppan has been afflicted from birth, will in all probability result in her death. . . . The world shuddered when Jane Toppan was arrested and her crimes were told in print. Dr. Stedman has evidence to substantiate twenty of the murders to which she confesses: the other eleven are beyond investigation. In two instances she claimed to have been seized with compunction and to have sent for another nurse. One of the patients was saved in consequence. In another instance she took the opportunity to repeat the dose and make sure of her victim . . . the case takes on a phase of extraordinary interest, not only to the medical and legal professions but to the layman.

—LOS ANGELES HERALD, NOVEMBER 6, 1904.

For years, nurses in the asylum would hear her calling down the halls, threatening to kill again. "Get some morphine, dearie, and we'll go out in the ward," she'd say. "You and I will have a lot of fun seeing them die."

—KATIE SERENA, "INSIDE THE TWISTED MIND AND MURDERS OF 'JOLLY' JANE TOPPAN," *ATI*, FEBRUARY 26, 2018.

CHAPTER 17

The American Jack the Ripper

Ameer Ben Ali, 1891

Called the American Jack the Ripper, Ameer Ben Ali, an Algerian immigrant, was found guilty of murder and sentenced to life imprisonment for the brutal murder of Carrie Brown.

On July 10, 1891, Ameer Ben Ali, an Algerian immigrant, was found guilty of second-degree murder and sentenced to life imprisonment for the brutal murder of Carrie Brown in a sensational case dubbed "The American Jack the Ripper." He spent eleven years incarcerated before New York Governor Benjamin B. Odell issued a pardon for him based on new and startling evidence that had come to light.

On the morning of Friday, April 24, 1891, James Jennings made his way up the narrow staircase to the fifth floor of the seedy East River Hotel along New York City's dangerous waterfront. When he reached the landing, he saw a trail of blood leading from Room 31. A blood-splattered floor was not an unusual sight for Jennings, who owned the rundown place, since the hotel was frequented by any number of riverfront thugs, sailors, and prostitutes. There were always drunken fights and stabbings, but this was different. There was too much blood, and it was everywhere. Jennings didn't bother to knock. He let himself in with a spare key. Jennings, who thought he had seen it all, was not squeamish, but what he discovered inside the room sickened him. Lying on the bed was the body of sixty-year-old Carrie Brown who was known to dole out her services regularly at the sleazy hotel. She had been disemboweled, her intestines spread across the bed and the floor. The killer had carved an X on her left thigh. A bloody wooden-handled knife was lying on the floor beside the bed. The point of the knife had been broken off. Jennings summoned the police.

Thomas Byrnes, chief inspector of the New York Police Department's Detective Bureau, raced over from the 300 Mulberry Street police headquarters. Under normal circumstances, the murder of a whore along the East River would barely get a rise out of Byrnes. Water Street was overflowing with cheap barrooms, dance halls, and sordid hotels where prostitutes and criminals nightly plied their trade. Murder and mayhem were a weekly, if not nightly, occurrence. The discovery of Brown's mutilated body would have been a routine incident for Byrnes, but he knew that this murder would likely be an albatross around his neck if he didn't solve it quickly. Six weeks before the Brown murder, *The New York Times* crime beat reporter asked Byrnes to comment on the ongoing Scotland Yard investigation of the infamous White Chapel killings—the unsolved murder and mutilation of East End London prostitutes that were attributed to Jack the Ripper. Byrnes boasted he would catch Jack the Ripper in two days if he ever struck in New York City, and now it appeared he would have to make good on his boast. Brown's murder had all the trappings of a Jack the Ripper killing.

Jack the Ripper was responsible for the murder and mutilation of at least five prostitutes during his killing spree in the East End of London in 1888, and no one was ever arrested or tried for the murders. The identity of the Ripper remains a mystery to this day. Jack the Ripper was the name given to the killer because of a series of letters sent to Scotland Yard from someone claiming to be the killer and signing the letters using that name. Following one brutal murder of Alice McKenzie in London in July 1889, it was thought that the Ripper had returned. Since the murders stopped as suddenly as they had begun, it was thought that the Ripper had died, had been captured for some other crime, or had gone to America to ply his gristly trade. The New York City press was more than happy to have its own Chief Inspector Byrnes show how to catch the Ripper in the good old-fashioned American way.

Byrnes was the right man for the job. The forty-nine-year-old Byrnes had grown up in dire poverty on the streets of New York City. He was a mostly self-educated, Irish immigrant who joined the police force in 1863 and rose through the ranks quickly, overcoming the era's bias against the Irish, by solving a series of highly publicized crimes. He was a master of self-promotion, never missing an opportunity to publicize his exploits and deeds. The cigar-chomping, often soft-spoken, detective was a powerfully built man with broad shoulders and meaty hands, who moved deftly, almost gracefully. He looked younger than his years, despite the huge handlebar mustache and sideburns speckled with gray.

Byrnes was credited with turning the Detective Bureau into one of the most efficient crime-fighting departments in the world through his innovative investigative methods. Byrnes was instrumental in the Detective Bureau's incorporation of intelligence gathering as a vital part of police work. He ordered detectives to keep and submit detailed notes of all their undercover activities and initiated the practice of photographing criminals when they were arrested. He was the first in American law enforcement to catalog criminal histories of felons in a central data bank, including photo albums of known criminals. Byrnes instituted the first "Rogues' Gallery," a photographic lineup of suspected criminals. He made sure that his detectives, nicknamed the immortals by the New York City press, kept up-to-date records on all known and suspected criminals. His detectives were depicted in the press as all-knowing, all-seeing public avengers who lurked behind every corner of the vast city. In 1886, Byrnes published *Professional Criminals of America*, a photojournalistic textbook on crime fighting, which became a must-read for police departments throughout the country. Byrnes's law enforcement innovations earned him the title "Father of the Modern Detective."

Byrnes was considered a master psychologist who knew just the right approach with each criminal brought before him for interrogation. Backed by his uncanny detection abilities, his all-encompassing files, and his shadowy detective force, Byrnes always seemed to get his man. The truth of this, of course, fell far short. Byrnes did in fact modernize New York's Detective Bureau, making it the model for every other big city police department, but the aura of an omnipotent detective force was an illusion that Byrnes carefully crafted. The press coverage of his often-brutal methods of interrogation popularized the term "the third degree," the use of psychological or physical torture to obtain a confession. Some writers maintained that Byrnes actually coined the phrase "the third degree."

Under Byrnes's direction, police searched the fifth floor of the hotel looking for anything that might help in the investigation. According to witnesses, Carrie Brown came to the hotel between 10:30 and 11:00 p.m. the night before. Brown, who was known as "Shakespeare," because she would often blurt out drunken recitations of *Hamlet* or *Macbeth*, claimed to have been a celebrated actress in England during her youth. Brown didn't sign the hotel register, but the man she had picked up signed in as "C. Knick." Mary Miniter, who worked as a housekeeper at the hotel, had caught a glimpse of the man accompanying Brown. Miniter told the police that the suspect tried to avoid being seen and that he turned away from her whenever she tried to get a better look at him.

Still, Miniter was steadfast in her claim that the man appeared to be a foreigner, youngish, and light-haired. Brown and the man were given the key to Room 31 on the fifth floor. While the detectives were searching the hotel for clues, the coroner began his preliminary examination of the body and reported that Brown had been strangled first and then mutilated. He publicly surmised to an eager throng of newspaper reporters the murder was done by the same person involved in London's White Chapel killings—Jack the Ripper. News of the murder swept across the city as special editions began flying off the presses. "CHOKED, THEN MUTILATED," screamed the banner headline of *The New York Times*. The *Tribune* ran with the sensational headline: JACK THE RIPPER STRIKES HOME. *The World* announced: RIPPER'S HORROR REPEATED AT EAST SIDE LODGING. None of the papers could resist running Byrnes's boast that if ever the Ripper came to New York, he'd have him behind bars within forty-eight hours.

Every available police officer and detective was assigned to the case. *The Times* later called the investigation "the greatest man hunt in the history of the city." Reports of the murder and the vague description of the murderer were distributed to all police stations and neighboring jurisdictions. There was a city wide dragnet for the suspected murderer. Police canvassed every hotel and lodging house along the waterfront. Byrnes ordered his men to apprehend any suspicious people they might encounter. Police went door to door in their systematic hunt for anyone who might have known Carrie Brown or had seen her before she checked into the East River Hotel with her killer. No one at the hotel had any memory of seeing C. Knick leaving the building that night or the following morning.

Police suspected that the killer had escaped through a skylight window on the roof and then run off undetected using an outside staircase. As the day wore on, uniformed police officers were positioned outside the entrance to the East River Hotel to keep the throngs of morbid curiosity seekers from entering and disturbing any evidence that might have been uncovered. Detectives went to Brown's Oliver Street lodging house, which was operated by Mamie Harrington. Harrington said Brown was drinking at the lodging house the night before with a man known "Frenchy" because he spoke with an accent that most people assumed was French. Her description of him was the same as the one Miniter had given to police. Back at the hotel, police learned that the suspect had taken Room 33 the night before, directly across the hall from Brown's room. Detectives now had a known suspect who had been seen with the mutilated victim only hours before her death.

A day following the murder, police arrested an Algerian immigrant named Ameer Ben Ali. He was known in and around the East River Hotel neighborhood as "Frenchy." When he was arrested, there was blood on his shirt and on his hands and fingernails. According to Ali, he had been in a fistfight the night before. At first, Ben Ali denied ever being near the hotel the night of the murder and denied any knowledge of Brown. He later recanted, some suspect because of Byrnes's persuasive third degree. Ali freely admitted to the police that after a bout of drinking, he had rented a room with Brown at the East River Hotel. He also admitted to being in the hotel at the time of Brown's murder. But he disavowed any involvement in it. Miniter was brought in to identify the suspect. She told police that Ben Ali was not the man who had rented the room at the hotel with Brown.

When informed of the disappointing news, Byrnes decided it didn't matter and kept Ben Ali locked up anyway as a material witness in the case. A succession of suspects was arrested, detained, questioned, and released. The police had cobbled together a scenario covering Carrie Brown's last few hours based on various reports given to them by various witnesses. What they knew was that Brown had been seen drinking with Ameer Ben Ali, who was still being held in custody but not charged. Brown and Ben Ali had been joined by another man. What the police learned about the second man was that he too spoke French and also went by the nickname Frenchy. He was Ben Ali's cousin. Police began the search for the second suspect.

It didn't take very long for the crazies to come out of the woodwork when the story broke in the newspapers. Police were deluged with false claims regarding the whereabouts of the suspected murderer. Ben Ali and his cousin were both sailors. Police spread out along the East River piers checking ships and manifests for Frenchy No. 2. They were not able to turn up the second suspect. By Monday, April 27, nearly four days after the murder, the police were still stymied but then there was a break in the case. The Queens County sheriff contacted Byrnes and informed him that he had evidence that, before being arrested as a material witness in the Brown murder, Ben Ali had been held at the Queens County jail where police confiscated a knife that had been in his possession.

Although the knife was no longer in the possession of the sheriff, because it had been returned to Ben Ali after he was released, Byrnes produced the wooden-handled knife that had been found at the crime scene. Although the knife the sheriff was shown was battered and bloodied and the tip of it broken off, the sheriff was sure it was the same knife that had been in the possession of Ben Ali. That was enough for Byrnes. He had his man.

Byrnes contacted the New York City Board of Health and had Dr. Cyrus Edson conduct several reportedly scientific examinations of blood found on Ben Ali's clothes and under his fingernails. Although Byrnes and Edson claimed the examination scientifically proved that the blood was human blood, there was no way to prove that it was the blood of Carrie Brown. It wasn't until 1900 that Karl Landsteiner, a professor of pathological anatomy at the University of Vienna, first discovered human blood groups. It was Landsteiner's discovery that allowed forensic scientists to identify various blood groups. Edson would not have been able to perform such an analysis prior to that time. As Byrnes intensified his investigation aimed at proving Ben Ali was Brown's murderer, he began to accumulate more circumstantial evidence, primarily dealing with Ben Ali's character.

Several sources came forward to claim that Ben Ali was a dangerous man who, on more than one occasion, had threatened and abused women, including Brown on the night she was murdered. Byrnes pointed out to reporters that Ben Ali was a merchant seaman who traveled back and forth between New York City and London, the operative word being London. In this way, Byrnes attempted to associate Ben Ali with the London-based Jack the Ripper. Byrnes proudly declared that Frenchy, Ameer Ben Ali, was the killer. The illustrious Chief of Detectives Thomas

Byrnes had gotten his man once again. The motive, according to Byrnes, was simple: money. Ben Ali had stolen what little money Brown had on her. The case was solved.

Ben Ali was arraigned and his trial began in early June. Byrnes and four officers testified for the prosecution. Dozens of denizens of the East River waterfront were called by the prosecution to testify against Ben Ali. Several medical experts were also called to testify. They all indicated that the blood found on Ben was consistent with blood found fundamentally in human intestines and consistent with the blood flowing from the gruesome abdominal injuries inflicted on Brown. Through his interpreter, Ben Ali denied killing Brown. The trial lasted less than a month, and on July 10, 1891, Ameer Ben Ali was found guilty of second-degree murder and sentenced to life imprisonment. Although the case was closed and Ben Ali was in prison, rumors about the murder persisted. Byrnes offered no explanation as to why Ben Ali would have disemboweled the aging prostitute, or how he could have mimicked the London Jack the Ripper cases since he couldn't read English and there was no way he could have read any American or English newspapers describing the crimes. Many, especially in the press, felt Ben Ali had been framed in order to save Byrnes's reputation as the city's preeminent crime fighter. Other facts in the case had also been conveniently ignored.

Although the case remained suspect, Ali remained in prison and Chief Detective Thomas Byrnes was once more heralded as New York City's top cop. However, based on new evidence, New York governor Benjamin B. Odell issued a pardon for Ameer Ben Ali in 1902. Ali had served nearly eleven years in prison. He was subsequently deported to Algeria. No investigation into the prosecution of Ben Ali was ever conducted, and the immaculate reputation of Byrnes remained untarnished. Byrnes had displayed a pioneering investigative technique in the Ben Ali case, attempting to connect Ali to the crime through the rudimentary examination of blood samples. Although his technique was flawed, the process remained a prototype for future forensic practice. Less than a year after the Ben Ali case, in April 1892, Byrnes was appointed superintendent of the New York City Police Department.

A murder which in many of its details recalls the crimes with which "Jack the Ripper" horrified London was committed late Thursday night or early yesterday morning in a small room in the squalid lodging house known as the East River Hotel, on the southeast corner of Catharine and Water Streets. The victim was an old, gray haired, and wrinkled woman, who had for years past haunted the neighborhood. The murderer escaped hours before the deed was discovered. He left behind him the weapon with which he had butchered his victim. . . . The police theory, however, is that "Jack" is not in New-York, but that an imitator, perhaps a crank, committed the murder. A strict policy of not saying a word about the case was kept up last night. At midnight the temporary detective headquarters at the Oak Street Station were closed for the night, but the night squad were told to look out for a man about 5 feet 8 inches high, rather thin, with a light moustache, light hair, and hooked nose, and dressed in a dark cutaway coat and derby hat.

—THE NEW YORK TIMES, APRIL 25, 1891.

There was no startling development in the East River Hotel murder yesterday. The police seem to be absolutely at sea. They will say nothing perhaps because they have nothing to say. They display an irritability that is in itself strong evidence that they are completely baffled. The official statement made by Inspector Byrnes late Saturday night to the effect that he was almost satisfied that the perpetrator of the crime was a man known as "Frenchy," a cousin of George Francis, also known as "Frenchy," the last named now being in the hands of the police. It is generally believed to have been what in police circles is called a "throwoff." Byrnes as much said he would be able to put his hands on Frenchy as soon as he wanted him. He has not got him yet. . . . Byrnes himself said yesterday that "Frenchy" had not been arrested. This and the statement that the description of the murderer were conflicting thus rendering identification extremely difficult were the only statements that the Inspector would make for publication. The manner in which the police are working is almost conclusive evidence that they are just where they started, so far as the actual capture of the murderer is concerned. They are simply pursuing a drag-net policy. . . . Mysteriously as the police are moving it is known that they made a number of arrests yesterday. Most of the prisoners, after examination were discharged."

—*THE NEW YORK TIMES*, APRIL 27, 1891.

CHAPTER 18

The Bicycle Bandit

Herbert Willis, 1896

Young Herbert Willis robbed stores wearing a mask and brandishing two revolvers and always managed to escape the authorities on a bicycle.

Herbert Willis, the twenty-year-old son of a prominent Taunton, Massachusetts, businessman, robbed stores throughout the southeastern Massachusetts region wearing a mask and brandishing two revolvers, and while he managed to elude police, escaping on a bicycle, his daring life of crime came to an abrupt end when he murdered teenager Fred Strange in an attempt to steal his bicycle.

It was a warm June night in 1896, in the small industrial city of Taunton, Massachusetts, located midway between Providence, Rhode Island, and Boston, Massachusetts. Nineteen-year-old Fred Strange and his friend Irvin Lincoln were riding their bicycles home from Memorial Park where the outdoor band concert had just ended. They stopped at the intersection of Winthrop and Highland Street. The two young men were best friends, graduating from high school together in 1894. They were bicycling enthusiasts and were founders and members of the Taunton Cycling Club. Bicycle clubs had sprung up all over the country in response to the bicycling craze that was sweeping the country. As Lincoln waited, out of the corner of his eye he caught a glimpse of someone riding a bicycle up Winthrop Street toward them at breakneck speed. The mysterious rider skidded to a stop in front of them. He wore a mask made out of dark fabric. Lincoln laughed, thinking it was some sort of a joke, but he stopped laughing when the masked man drew a gun, pointed it at the two men, and demanded Lincoln's new bike. Fred Strange would have none of it. He leapt at the man and tried to grab the gun away from him. The gun went off, hitting Strange in the stomach. He fell to the ground mortally wounded. The masked bandit grabbed Lincoln's bike and rode off in the direction of Providence.

The sound of the gunshot woke people and a crowd gathered on the sidewalk. Several people helped lift Stranger's limp body out of the street. He was unconscious when he was brought by ambulance to Morton Hospital in downtown Taunton, approximately two miles away. At the hospital, he was attended to by several physicians. His parents were called. Despite several attempts to retrieve the bullet, he died without regaining consciousness on June 25, three days after the shooting. The funeral for

Fred Strange was held at his family home. Hundreds of people, including members of the Taunton Cycle Club, turned out.

The Strange family offered a $500 reward for the capture of their son's murderer and the local newspaper, the *Taunton Daily Gazette*, matched the amount. Although the Taunton police conducted a thorough investigation, interrogating everyone remotely connected to the case, they didn't turn up a single clue. A reward poster was issued and circulated throughout Taunton and the surrounding towns, all the way to Rhode Island, twenty miles away. The only thing the police had to go on was the description and make of the bicycle that the masked bandit had stolen from Lincoln. Despite all the best efforts by the Taunton police, the $1,000 reward and even a massive search conducted by the Taunton Cycle Club, Strange's killer remained at large. It was as if the ground had swallowed up the mysterious masked bicycle bandit. Ironically, it had.

The month of July passed without any further developments in the Strange murder case, but the city and surrounding towns were beset by a series of unsolved burglaries and highway robberies. Two stores in the adjacent town of Raynham were robbed in broad daylight by a man wearing a mask and brandishing two guns. A store in the Oakland section of the City of Taunton was robbed, but not at gunpoint: someone broke into the store at night and stole an assortment of merchandise. Police surmised it was the work of the same person—a bold and dangerous young man who made his getaways on a bicycle. The police dubbed the unknown culprit "The Bicycle Bandit."

The bandit made his way to Rhode Island and, in mid-July, he robbed yet another bicycle from a young man at gunpoint. The victim reported the theft to police. The police caught up with the bandit who was attempting to escape on the bicycle. The police were chasing him on foot. The bandit discarded the bicycle and tried to escape on foot. He drew his gun on police but was subdued when one of the officers hit him over the head with his night stick, sending the bandit sprawling to the ground. But not even the blow to the head could stop him. He jumped to his feet, broke free of the two police officers, jumped a fence, and disappeared. At the very least, the police now had a description of the bandit. Providence police issued a description of the bandit identifying the suspect as a young man approximately five feet ten inches tall, with a slim build, weighing about 160 pounds with black hair, a dark tanned complexion, and very white and even teeth. When word of the incident reached the Taunton police, they were sure that the Rhode Island bandit and the murderer of Fred Strange were one and the same.

And then there was the shootout. On Wednesday morning, July 29, 1896, in downtown Providence, a young man walked into the sporting goods store of James Dawson with a bicycle he wanted to sell. The man matched the description of the bandit Rhode Island and Taunton police were after. Dawson made sure his revolver below the cash register was within reach. The young man made no attempt to rob the store. Instead, he offered to trade his bicycle for some merchandise. Dawson examined the bicycle and discovered that the bicycle had been stolen in Taunton. Dawson slipped to the front of the store and locked the door. Dawson told the young man he was holding him until the police arrived. The young man became enraged. He reached inside his coat and drew two pistols. Dawson was already one step ahead of him. He had gone behind the counter and pulled his own revolver on the man. What the young man couldn't have known was that the gun that Dawson had trained on him wasn't loaded. It didn't matter. He made a break for it.

The bandit darted to the front of the store, grabbed several baseball bats, and, in full view of people passing by on the sidewalk outside, smashed the plate glass window of Dawson's store and dove through the shattered glass, cutting his hands. Without looking back, he jumped on another bicycle he had parked outside and raced off. Dawson chased after him yelling for someone to stop him. Two men standing on the corner of the busy street jumped in front of him and knocked him to the ground. The bandit jumped to his feet and began firing at the two men. One was shot in the leg. The other ducked behind cover. A wild shot hit an innocent bystander. Dawson, who was in hot pursuit, this time with a loaded gun, fired several shots but missed. The bandit raced down the street on foot, guns blazing. A crowd of men and police were now in hot pursuit, but the bandit managed to escape again.

He stole another bicycle and headed back to Taunton. Providence police contacted the Taunton police and told them to be on the lookout for the bandit heading up Winthrop Street toward Taunton. Taunton police set up what they thought would be a foolproof roadblock. The officers tied a length of clothesline to a tree on one side of Winthrop Street and laid it across the street. The two officers next hid in the woods on the opposite side of the street with the free end of the clothesline in their grip. It was well past midnight when the bicycle bandit came riding hard up Winthrop Street and raced pass the clothesline roadblock, before the police could pull the line tight. The bicycle bandit once again successfully eluded his pursuers and vanished into thin air.

It was a chance meeting that ultimately led to the arrest of the bandit. Two young men ran into Herbert Willis at the Willis Fish Market on Weir Street in Taunton. Herbert, the twenty-year-old son of a prominent Taunton businessman, Samuel Willis, worked in the store. By everyone's account, he was a friendly, polite, hardworking young man who was seemingly devoted to his family and who attended church regularly. It was hard to believe that Herbert Willis could possibly be the now infamous "Bicycle Bandit." The two men saw cuts on Willis's hands, wounds the bandit had gotten from jumping through Dawson's plate glass window. They became suspicious when they asked Willis what had happened to his hands and Willis responded that he had accidentally cut himself while sharpening a knife in his father's store. Willis had told others an entirely different story when asked about the cuts.

On the morning of August 8, a detachment of four Taunton police officers descended on the Willis Fish Market to confront Willis. According to a *Taunton Daily Gazette* news story, what transpired next was "the most desperate struggle that ever took place during the arrest of a criminal in this city."

Willis was tending the store alone when the police walked in. They told him they were taking him to police headquarters for questioning. Willis asked to excuse himself so that he could change out of his fishy-smelling clothes. He went into the back room. Suddenly, Willis came bounding out of the backroom with two guns blazing, bullets flying in every direction. Luckily, none of the officers were hit. The four officers managed to wrestle the guns from Willis and subdue him after grappling in hand-to-hand combat. Immediately following Willis's arrest police searched Willis's home. They found a stash of stolen merchandise hidden in Willis's room, including several pistols, cigars, candy, pocketbooks, cash, and a host of other stolen items. The stash was identified as having been stolen during the recent rash of store robberies. No one, including his own father, could fathom Herbert's life of crime and certainly not his being the masked bandit that shot and killed Fred Strange. The stolen merchandise found at the Willis's home was merely the tip of the iceberg. During questioning, Willis, who basked in his criminal notoriety, told police they could find more stolen loot in a cave he had dug in a field along Winthrop Street, not far from the place where Strange was killed. When police found the cave, they discovered it was nearly ten feet deep with a sloping tunnel, big enough only for a bicycle leading into it. The tall grass and brush hid the dirt ramp into the cave from view. Willis told police that many times he eluded the police by disappearing down the ramp into the safety of his underground hideout. Inside the cave, police discovered an incredible stash of stolen merchandize, including several bicycles and guns. They reported there was enough to fill a wagon.

During further questioning by the police, Willis said he wanted to get it off his chest and confessed that he had shot and killed Fred Strange. Willis's trial began in February 1897. He pled not guilty, despite his confession. The courthouse was packed with news reporters, city officials, family, and curiosity seekers. Willis continued to bask in his infamy, freely talking to newspaper reporters, telling them of the many robberies and burglaries he had committed and how he had eluded police for so long. A number of witnesses were called to testify to Willis's abhorrent behavior. Dr. Samuel Abbott, who had treated Willis as a patient, called Willis "erratic and crack-brained." Abbott told the court that he thought Willis's brain had been addled by reading too many lurid dime novels. The police confirmed that a large number of dime novels about bandits, robberies, and daredevil escapes had been found in Willis's home and his hideout. Emma Brown, a young woman that Willis had known, told the court that Willis had promised to get her a new bicycle, "just like Diamond Jim gave to Lillian Russell." She said that Willis did once show up at her home with a brand new bicycle for her but that she refused the gift and that he became angry and stormed off.

Willis ultimately was persuaded by his attorney to change his plea from not guilty of first-degree murder to guilty of murder in the second degree in order to escape the potential death penalty. The trial lasted less than an hour and Willis was sentenced to life imprisonment at Charlestown jail. His most frequent visitor while he was in jail was his younger brother, seventeen-year-old Everett Willis. Everett idolized his older brother. Newspaper and magazines and even dime novels now told stories about the exploits of the daredevil Bicycle Bandit, Herbert Willis. Herbert was famous.

On Tuesday, August 10, 1897, Everett Willis managed to smuggle several guns into the jail to help his brother escape. The two young men met in the prison visiting room watched over by a guard. When visiting hours were over, Everett pulled gun on the guard and demanded he unlock the door. At the same time, he tossed two guns to his brother.

The guard reached for his gun and Herbert Willis fired several shots at him hitting the guard in the arm and leg. Other guards rushed to the scene. Several of the doors leading to room burst open and officers flooded into the room. Herbert Willis fired randomly at them. Officers fired back. Herbert Willis was hit in the in the arm, throat, head, and back in the fusillade. It was estimated than more than thirty rounds of ammunition were fired between the Willis Brothers and the jail officers. When the smoke finally cleared, Herbert Willis was lying face down on the floor mortally wounded and Everett Willis had been shot three times. Only one guard had been shot. The entire shootout lasted less than three minutes.

Herbert Willis was taken to the prison infirmary and Everett was taken to Massachusetts General Hospital to be treated for his wounds. After the shootout, police discovered two bicycles concealed in the bushes near the Charlestown Jail, apparently stashed there by Everett to be used in the planned escape. Police later discovered that both bicycles had been stolen.

Herbert Willis died three days after his attempted jailbreak without gaining consciousness. Everett Willis recovered from his wounds and was to sentenced fifteen years of hard labor. He was released from prison in 1912 and never heard from again. Herbert Willis, the infamous Bicycle

Bandit, was buried in the Willis family plot in Bristol Rhode Island's North Cemetery. He was only twenty-one years old when he died. Willis told newspaper reporters, "Some people are bad all their lives, but my wickedness seemed to break out all at once." For Herbert Willis, the "all at once" was now over.

Everett Willis was seriously wounded in the attempt to help his brother Herbert escape from state prison, but a month later he was well enough to be arraigned in Suffolk County Superior Court on two counts of assault with intent to kill, one for each of the prison guards who had been most seriously injured in the shoot-out. Only 17-years old and intending to plead guilty at trial, Everett refused to allow his mother to hire a lawyer to defend him, and he awaited his day in court in a cell at the Charles Street Jail in downtown Boston.

—Old Colony History Museum, "The Bicycle Bandit
and the Brother Who Loved Him," March 15, 2018.

He Is only nineteen years but he has blood on his hands and a record of daring crimes that would make him respected in the company of notorious desperados. . . . On a bicycle he affected those reported mysterious escapes that for months kept his identity secret. . . . On the night of June 22 he began his career of blood with the murder of and the robbery of his friends. . . . Both Strange and Lincoln were acquaintances from that time till when he was arrested after a terrible struggle with four police. He committed several crimes each week and secured a large amount of plunder which he secreted in a cave.

—New York World, September 13, 1896.

CHAPTER 19

Murder of an Angelic Songbird

Clarence Richeson, 1911

Massachusetts minister Clarence Richeson poisoned his fiancé Avis Linnell so he could marry another woman.

Clarence Richeson, a Cambridge, Massachusetts, minister, thought he had forever silenced the beautiful, young, songbird he had seduced and abandoned, but even in death, her voice rang true, ending his deceitful plans for attaining wealth and status at any price.

IN OCTOBER 1911, AVIS LINNELL, A NINETEEN-YEAR-OLD MUSIC STUDENT from Hyannis, Massachusetts, was found dead in the bathroom at the Boston Young Woman's Catholic Association (YWCA) where she was living. Her body was found on the floor of the bathroom. She died before an ambulance could be called. Her death was initially ruled a suicide because she was depressed over her broken wedding engagement to a minister named Clarence Richeson. There was no initial suspicion of foul play even though the postmortem examination found potassium cyanide in her body. The autopsy also revealed that she was pregnant, which indicated to the authorities that she had killed herself to cover up her condition. Several hours after she died, a YWCA matron called Reverend Richeson to tell him what happened. He had been previously engaged to Linnell, but he told the matron he barely knew the girl. He demanded to know why he was called. After denying that he knew her, he asked "Why did you phone me? Tell her parents." The matron, who was already suspicious given Richeson's initial reaction, informed him that she knew he had lunch with Linnell earlier that day because Linnell had told her about it. Richeson denied meeting with her. At the end of conversation, he asked, "Did she say anything before she died?"

Linnell was born in Hyannis Port on Cape Cod in 1891 and graduated from high school in 1908 and later from Normal School in 1910. A normal school was an institution of higher learning dedicated to training women to become teachers.

According to a newspaper article in the Cape Cod *Sandwich Observer*, in 1911, she had "an exceedingly bright intellect which carried her through school with ease." She had an exquisite soprano singing voice and was described in the local newspaper as an "angelic songbird." She sang in the choir at the small Baptist church in Hyannis that she attended with her parents and three sisters.

In 1908, Richeson became the minister at Linnell's church. He was a tall, handsome, charismatic man, originally from Virginia, and Linnell was instantly taken with him. It appeared he was in love with her as well. He was twelve years older than her. On her nineteenth birthday, he proposed marriage and gave her a ring.

In 1899, Richeson entered the William Jewell College in Liberty, Missouri. He later matriculated at the Southern Baptist Seminary in Louisville, Kentucky, and was ordained as a Baptist minister at the Third Baptist church while still a student, and he became preacher at the Budd Park Baptist Church in Kansas City from 1901 to 1904. The trustees asked for his resignation after he allegedly proposed to three girls. He also preached at a mission church at Kansas City. While still in school, in 1905, he was expelled for cheating. An official at the college wrote his father stating, "Clarence had become deranged," and they could no longer keep him as a student.

In 1906, Richeson entered the Newton Theological Seminary in Newton, Massachusetts, and finally graduated in 1909. He accepted a position at the small Baptist church in Hyannis but his preaching style was far too spirited for the conservative members of the Hyannis church and he was forced to resign in 1910. He moved to Cambridge, Massachusetts, where he was hired by the Immanuel Baptist Church. He persuaded Avis Linnell, whom he had met and wooed at the Hyannis church, to apply to the New England Conservatory of Music in Boston, which she did and in the fall of 1910, she moved into the Boston YWCA. The date for her marriage to Richeson was set for October 1910. She wore the engagement ring until Christmas 1910 and after he broke off their engagement, she gave it back to Richeson.

In early 1911, Avis wrote to her mother that she and Richeson had broken off their engagement, and in March, Richeson announced his engagement to Violet Edmands, a wealthy young woman from Brookline, Massachusetts. As his relationship with Violet Edmands became more serious, Richeson attempted to distance himself from Linnell. Using the excuse that the diamond in her ring was loose, he took the engagement ring back from her reportedly to be repaired, but she never received the ring back.

Richeson first met Violet and Rose Edmands in 1907. Violet and Rose were the only two children of Moses Grant Edmands and his wife Lydia. He referred to his wife and daughters as his three flowers. Violet and Richeson began seeing each other weekly from December 1910, until their engagement was announced in March. *The Patriot*, a Cape Cod newspaper, published the announcement of Richeson's engagement to Edmands on March 13, 1911, but in July, he returned to Hyannis where he resumed his relationship with Avis over the summer. It was in July of that year that she reportedly became pregnant. Although friends and family knew their engagement had been broken off, they readily assumed that the young couple had renewed their engagement because of how much time they spent together. At the end of that summer, Richeson returned to resume his duties at the Immanuel Baptist Church in Cambridge and Avis returned to her studies at the New England Conservatory of Music in Boston and her room at the YWCA.

The date set for the marriage between Richeson and Edmands was October 31, 1911, but his marriage plans began to fall apart shortly after the engagement was announced when Linnell revealed to him that she was pregnant. Richeson immediately began to take steps to remedy the situation. "How long ago he learned of the girl's condition can never be known, for the girl did not even take her mother into her confidence," the chief inspector in the case, Joseph Dugan, said. "But we do know that when the formal invitations to his marriage of Miss Edmands were sent out. . . . Miss Linnell's condition was desperate."

Edwin Grozier, the editor of the *Boston Post*, became suspicious of Richeson after he learned that Richeson had denied knowing Linnell. The *Post* demanded a police investigation into Linnell's death and the medical examiner, Dr. Timothy Leary, ultimately ruled that Linnell's death was not a suicide. He assigned several reporters on the story and they discovered that Richeson had bought cyanide from a druggist in Newton, Massachusetts.

The press and police both started digging into the claim. They scoured the Newton neighborhood searching for leads and ultimately located druggist William Hahn, whose shop was located in Newton Center. Hahn told detectives that one of his regular customers had come to him a short time earlier with an unusual request. The customer was Richeson. He told the druggist that he had a dog who was going to have puppies, and that he wanted to kill her. Hahn suggested chloroform, but Richeson said he wanted something quicker. Hahn poured out enough cyanide to kill ten dogs. Richeson asked for more.

"I gave him enough to kill 10 people," Hahn told investigators. The cyanide capsules were purchased on October 10. Four days later, Linnell was dead from cyanide poisoning.

The police questioned Richeson's landlord asking if he owned a dog. He didn't. There was only one dog in the house, a male, and he belonged to the landlord. Police also found cyanide capsules hidden in Richeson's room.

According to police reports, Richeson met with Linnell over lunch the day she died and gave her a vial of medicine that he said would cause an abortion. He had given her enough poison to kill "ten people." He was convinced people would conclude that heartbroken Linnell had taken her own life because he had broken off their engagement and because of his subsequent engagement to Edmands. What his reprehensible undertaking did not consider was the likelihood of an autopsy, which would not only reveal the presence of poison but would show she was pregnant. Even more damning was the fact that he did not envision she would tell friends at the YWCA that she had had lunch with him and that he had given her some "headache medicine." At the same time when the druggist Hahn was telling police that he sold cyanide to Richeson, the minister fled his lodgings and took refuge at the Edmands' home. Both Moses Edmands and his daughter expressed their support for Richeson to the police investigators who desperately wanted to speak to the minister.

The news of Richeson's crime spread quickly and throngs of newspapermen surrounded the Edmands home, where Richeson was hiding. They didn't get an interview, but later in the day, the police demanded to meet with Moses Edmands to no avail. The newspapermen and the police waited outside the house through the night and in the morning Edmands finally came to the door and reluctantly escorted the lawmen to the room where Richeson was lying in bed, still in his pajamas. They arrested him for the murder of Avis Linnell, and he was taken to the Charles Street Jail in Boston.

On October 31, the day he was to be married, Richeson was indicted. Violet Edmands fled Cambridge and went into hiding. Her family began returning the wedding gifts that had been delivered. No one could believe the charge against him. Members of his congregation remained steadfast in their belief that Richeson would be proven not guilty. The Edmands family also stood by him and the elder Edmands agreed to pay for his legal defense.

The prosecution's theory was that Richeson had given Linnell the poison, telling the desperate girl that it would end her pregnancy and avoid a scandal. The prosecution's case remained circumstantial. No one had seen him give her the cyanide capsules and no one had seen him with Linnell on the day of her murder. This made the YMCA's matron's testimony hearsay evidence. She never saw them together and only knew what Linnell had told her of the meeting.

A grand jury brought an indictment on November 2 containing five counts saying he had bought the poison with the intent of giving it to Linnell; that he gave Linnell the poison; he caused her to take the poison; he gave her the poison pretending it was a medical preparation; and he did "assault and poison with intent to murder by this giving and causing to be taken." He was arraigned and pleaded not guilty on November 13. The trial was set for January 15, 1912. Violet Edmands never once visited him in jail during his incarceration.

On December 20, 1911, while still being held in jail, Richeson mutilated his genitals using a piece of metal he had hidden in his cell. Although the injuries were not life-threatening, doctors were not able to save his penis and decidedly completed the job Richeson had started. It remained uncertain whether Richeson planned to commit suicide or was merely punishing himself for his sins. His lawyers sought clemency on the basis of insanity. Richeson had "delusions, hallucinations, amnesic periods, and delirium," according to Dr. Vernon Briggs, director of the Massachusetts Society for Mental Hygiene, who examined him.

"He had exhibited signs and had had attacks of this disease for years, had been recognized as mentally unsound by several physicians who advised specialists in mental diseases to attend him."

Ultimately, no jury was ever selected in the case. On January 5, Richeson retracted his not guilty plea and pleaded guilty to murder in the first degree. On January 12, 1912, he signed a written confession admitting he had killed Linnell by giving her capsules laced with cyanide. He told Linnell the capsules would induce an abortion. He was indicted and sentenced to die in the electric chair. Richeson told his attorney that he had to "set himself right with God."

The judge in the matter had no sentencing options other than death. The date for electrocution was set for May 19. Only after sentencing did his lawyers raise the question of insanity. The elder Edmands continued to offer support, saying he would spend whatever it took to get the sentence commuted. Attorneys appealed to the governor for clemency on the grounds of insanity, but the plea fell on deaf ears. Nothing could save Richeson.

He was executed in the electric chair on May 21, 1912 at 12:17 a.m. More than 2,000 people stood outside the prison walls for hours in pouring rain to attend the execution. The crowds outside the prison were so large that the outer gates were closed to prevent them from trespassing on the prison grounds and a special police unit was assigned for crowd control.

Before his death, Richeson told the prison guards who strapped him into the chair, "I have made peace with God. I am resigned to my fate. Quicker death, the better."

All the newspapers, including *The New York Times*, *Boston Globe*, *New York Daily Post*, and, of course, Edwin Grozier's *Boston Post*, gave the execution extensive overage. Author Theodore Dreiser wrote several chapters of a novel based on the murder but abandoned it to write about another murder: the 1906 murder of a factory girl, Grace Brown, by the factory owner, Chester Gillette. The similarities between the two cases were remarkable; both victims were young women seduced by older men and both were pregnant when they were murdered. It became the basis of Dreiser's most famous novel, *An American Tragedy* (1925).

The Edmands left Brookline, Massachusetts, and moved to Pasadena, California. Violet Edmands moved to New York City, where, under an assumed name, she dedicated her life to working with underprivileged children. She later moved to Japan, where she worked as a missionary. She returned to New York City years later, where she continued her work among the poor until her death at fifty-four in 1939. She never married.

Avis Linnell was buried in her family plot in Hyannis, Massachusetts. She was buried in the gown she made for her wedding. Richeson was buried near his family home in Virginia.

> *It was reported that Richeson had offered his jailers $100 at two different times to buy and bring poison to him. When I asked Sheriff Quinn if the report was true he answered "I had reason to suspect Richeson was preparing to commit suicide a few days ago (in May, 1912) and I removed everything from his cell and placed him in another cell by himself. After his removal he gave a blank stare at first and then went to pieces, became noisy and violent and had great difficulty in getting his breath. . . ." Immediately following the reading by his spiritual advisers of further quotations from the* Bible, *Richeson said: "This is Sunday my last on earth. If I had lived a righteous life, I should today be delivering a sermon from the pulpit of my church in Cambridge instead of being caged here awaiting a felon's death. But although I have sinned greatly, God is with me. For I have deeply repented. I feel that it is fitting, indeed I feel that it is my duty to offer up a sermon before I die and this my last Sunday is the proper day."*
>
> —L. VERNON BRIGGS, *THE MANNER OF MAN THAT KILLS*, 1921.

CHAPTER 20

Criminal Sweetheart

Sophie Lyons, 1913

Beautiful, smart, and daring, Sophie Lyons was one of the country's most notorious criminals for nearly fifty years.

Beautiful, smart, and daring, Sophie Lyons was one of the country's most notorious criminals for nearly fifty years, but in 1913, she renounced her life of crime and vowed to devote herself to helping criminals get back on the straight and narrow, but by then it was too late and her past caught up with her.

SOPHIE LYONS WAS IRRESISTIBLE TO MEN BECAUSE OF HER BEAUTY, CHARM, and intelligence.

She made her debut as a blackmailer in Boston sometime in the late 1870s. After being released from prison on a larceny charge in 1876, Lyons worked in Boston with her partner, Kate Leary, who was another known confidence woman. But her scam wasn't perfect. There, using her good looks and ample charms, she lured a wealthy businessman up to her hotel room. While the unsuspecting "mark" was undressing in the bathroom, she took his clothes and threatened to expose him if he did not make out a check in the amount of $10,000 and give it to her waiting accomplice, Leary, who was just outside the door to the room. Not wanting to be caught in such an indelicate situation, he wrote out the check as Lyons asked. Leary took the check immediately to the bank to cash it but when the check bounced, she was held by the police. During questioning, she revealed the whereabouts of Lyons and the captive businessman. The police went to the hotel where they arrested Lyons and released the embarrassed businessman. For obvious reasons the victim refused to appear in court to press charges against Lyons or Leary, and they were released from custody. Although his money was saved, his reputation and his marriage were ruined.

Sophie (Levy) Lyons was an American career criminal and one of the country's most notorious female thief, shoplifter, pickpocket, and confidence woman during the late 1800s. She was born in 1848 in New York City. Her father was a notorious burglar and her mother was a renowned pickpocket and shoplifter. She stole her first purse before she was six years old and was first arrested when she was twelve. She was punished by her stepmother if she did not steal enough.

Often her parents served jail terms simultaneously, leaving her to fend for herself. It was when her parents were both serving prison terms she came under the tutelage of Fredericka "Marm" Mandelbaum. Mandelbaum was the head of one of the biggest criminal syndicates in New York City during the Gilded Age. She was sent to Mandelbaum's school for little criminals on Grand Street and quickly became Mandelbaum's star pupil.

Sophie was an attractive young girl when she first met Mandelbaum, and Mandelbaum encouraged her to use her good looks in a series of immoral and criminal endeavors. She was victimized first by her abusive parents and then by Mandelbaum. Lyons had met Mandelbaum when she was a teenager and was molded by her. During the 1860s and 1870s, she became part of the inner circle of Mandelbaum's cadre of pickpockets, thieves, burglars, and confidence women. According to Herbert Asbury's seminal work *The Gangs of New York: An Informal History of the Underworld* (1928), Sophie Lyons was "perhaps the most notorious confidence woman America has ever produced." A confidence man (or woman) engages in defrauding people by gaining their trust and promising them some significant financial gain for placing their trust in them.

Sophie was, according to reports, "beautiful when young, and the traces never quite rubbed off." She was a consummate actress, could be demure when it best fitted the circumstances, or she could assume a lofty manner. She could weep or smile, as she chose. Her beauty, charm, and intelligence made her irresistible to men.

Sophie was married four times. She was first married in 1864 at sixteen years to Maury Harris, a professional pickpocket, who claimed to be the best in the business. Harris, however, was not as good as he thought. On their honeymoon, the police caught him red-handed trying to steal a wallet. He was arrested and sentenced to New York State Prison for two years. While Harris was in prison, she took up with Edward "Ned" Lyons, a notorious bank burglar.

Sophie met Ned Lyons at one of Mandelbaum's many dinner parties. At the party, Sophie stole a gold watch and diamond stickpin from another thief and gave them as a gift to Lyons. It made the right impression, and they were married shortly after their first meeting. It is not known whether Sophie obtained a legal divorce from Maury Harris before marrying Lyons. It didn't matter since there was no way Harris would go up against someone as powerful and dangerous as Lyons.

After they were married, Ned Lyons bought a home for her on Long Island and demanded that she give up her life of crime and dedicate herself to being a wife and mother. Initially, Sophie embraced her new life of domesticity. She became pregnant and gave birth to her first child, George. For a time, she was happy in her newfound familial role. It didn't last long. She missed the action. When George was only a few months old, she resumed her former vocation.

While Ned was away, occupied in one robbery or another, she went to Manhattan, where she plied her trade as a shoplifter and pickpocket. According to New York police detective Thomas Byrnes, she had a "mania for stealing was so strong that, when in Ned's company, she plied her vocation unknown to him, and would surprise him with watches, et cetera, which she had stolen." Her first born, George, turned to a life of crime in later life and spent much of his young life in and out of jail. He eventually died in prison, preceding his mother's death. In 1870, she was arrested for trying to steal diamonds from a jewelry shop and was sent to Sing Sing prison. Her husband had been previously arrested and sent to the same prison. Using her feminine wiles, she was able to get her hands on a prison pass from one of the guards, along with a change of clothes and was able to help her husband break out of prison. Ned Lyons then broke his wife out shortly afterward by secreting a key he had made from a wax mold. The couple fled to Canada.

In 1876, the couple were again arrested and sent back to Sing Sing to serve out their terms. This time there was no escape for either of them. Sophie was released first. While Ned was still serving out the rest of his prison term, Sophie decided to divorce him. Not only beautiful and charming, she was a talented actress, a trait that came in handy when she would lure some unsuspecting jewelry store or bank clerk into her web of larceny. In later life, she assumed the lofty role of a cultured lady of high society. No one was ever the wiser.

Sophie was credited with being the first defendant to use the "kleptomaniac" defense, before a jury. Her attorney had her break into sobs as she recounted for the jury how her compulsive thievery was the result of her abusive upbringing at the hands of a family of criminals. The jury bought her alligator tears and her poor, abused child routine and set her free.

Sophie managed to elude arrest on many occasions. During one incident, she was caught stealing red-handed by police who were besides themselves that they had finally apprehended the notorious Sophie Lyons. She managed to talk the police out of arresting her by claiming that the real Sophie Lyons would have been too smart to have been caught by such a bunch of inept police officers. She reportedly told police, "Sophie Lyons is a hardened criminal, and too smart to be caught like this." It worked. She wasn't arrested but was summarily escorted out of town.

While Ned Lyons was still in prison, she married a much younger, more handsome thief, Billie Burke. She and her new husband entered into a series of bank robberies. Sophie would act as a decoy distracting bank clerks or guards, once claiming to have fallen just outside the bank's front door and while the bank clerk and guard rushed to help her, Burke snuck inside and cleaned out the cash drawers. Their partnership became so successful that she and Burke were able to afford a home in Manhattan, a villa on the Riviera, and even a ranch out West.

The couple moved to Paris, where they hobnobbed with royalty and only society's upper crust. She hired tutors to help her learn languages, art, music, and history, allowing her to pass herself off as a cultured lady of exquisite taste and upbringing. She assumed the nom de plume of Madame de Varney. Using their many high society connections, she and Burke were able to engage in a slew of undetected robberies.

They were finally exposed as charlatans in Paris and elsewhere in Europe, when they were caught red-handed trying to steal a diamond necklace from one of her many upper crust friend's bedrooms during a gala party. She and Burke moved back to America and settled in Detroit. One of Detroit's many attractions was that it was not far from Canada, which did not have an extradition treaty with the United States. Criminals charged in Detroit could easily cross the border into Canada without fear of being returned.

When Ned Lyons was finally released from prison, he attempted to kill Billie Burke in a jealous rage. Lyons got the worst of it and was shot twice in the chest but survived. Burke was unharmed. Lyons was never able to assume his former place among New York City's criminal elite. He was arrested several more times and finally died in prison.

Sophie and Burke plied their criminal trade in Detroit for a time, but in early 1883, she was arrested and sentenced to three years in the Detroit House of Correction for larceny. When she was finally released in 1886, after a more than twenty-year life of crime, she made a life-changing decision. She had become too well known. She was getting older and she could not rely on her former beauty to slip out of trouble. In her early forties, she had spent almost a quarter of her life behind bars. It was time to quit her life of crime and she did.

Sophie had been a horrible mother and tried to redeem herself. She reportedly had nine children by five different fathers. Most of them had been placed into orphanages or convents at one time or another. Her two oldest sons had become career criminals. Her daughters were luckier than her sons. One daughter became a noted opera singer in Paris. Another lived in London. Her youngest daughter, who lived in Detroit, became a homeless beggar. In the end, however, she wound up as the major beneficiary of Sophie's will, making her a very wealthy woman. Her taste for the criminal life diminished and she moved back to Detroit, where she became a wealthy real estate investor. In 1913, she published her tell-all book, *Why Crime Does Not Pay*. She devoted most of her remaining life to helping other criminals and caring for her ailing husband.

Sophie worked with former prisoners, helping them to find work and providing food, shelter, and clothing. She became involved with a welfare organization called the Pathfinders and in prison reform. She helped start a home where preschool children could stay while their parents were in jail. In 1897, she became one of the first society gossip columnists in the country, writing for the *New York World* and became a Detroit real estate magnate, making a small fortune buying and selling homes and businesses in the city. She dedicated her life and fortune to funding prison reform and donating to libraries and orphanages. She tried to help ex-convicts get back on their feet, including her husband Billie Burke who had been released from prison in Stockholm and came back home to live with her.

Burke died in 1919 and Sophie continued with her philanthropic efforts. She donated land worth $35,000 to build a home where young children could live while their parents were serving sentences in prison. Her philanthropic work came to a bitter end on May 8, 1924, when two thieves that she had been trying to reform visited her at her home and demanded her money and jewels. When she refused, they pistol whipped her. She died of head injuries at the age of seventy-five. She was cremated and her ashes were placed in her son's grave at Woodmere Cemetery in Detroit.

For twenty-five years she lived on the proceeds of other people's crimes. During that time she made many millions. But these millions slipped away for the most part in bribing, fixing, and silencing people. Still she was a very wealthy, fat, ugly old woman when the blow fell.
        —SOPHIE LYONS, *WHY CRIME DOES NOT PAY*, 1913.

She was beautiful when young, and the traces never quite rubbed off. . . . Her features were regular and chiseled into a well-shaped oval face. Her eyes were an indeterminate gray-blue, and her almost-blond hair was piled on top of her head. She was a consummate actress, could be demure when it best fitted the circumstances, or she could assume the grand and lofty manner. She could weep or smile, as she chose. She wore dresses trimmed in laces and rich embroideries.
        —RICHARD BAK, "FROM ROGUE TO REFORMER," 2009.

MRS. SOPHIE BURKE, property owner, is dead in Detroit . . . leaving to charity a fortune (including jewelry) worth anywhere from $200,000 up—some say $1,000,000. That is the end of Sophie Lyons.
        —*THE NEW YORK TIMES*, MAY 18, 1924.

Further Reading and Sources

Abelson, Elaine S. *When Ladies Go A-Thieving: Middle-Class Shoplifters in the Victorian Department Store*, 1989.

Alix, Ernest Kahlar. *Ransom Kidnapping in America, 1874–1974: The Creation of a Capital Crime*, 1978.

Asbury, Herbert. *The Gangs of New York*, 1928.

An Authentic Biography of the Late Helen Jewett, A Girl of the Town by a Gentleman Fully Acquainted with Her History, 1836.

Avery, Ephraim and Richard Hildreth. *A Report of the Trial of the Rev. Ephraim K. Avery, before the Supreme Judicial Court of Rhode Island, on an Indictment for the Murder of Sarah Maria Cornell*, 1833.

Bates, Stephen. *The Poisoner: The Life and Crimes of Victorian England's Most Notorious Doctor*, 2014.

Beard, William Randall. "Women Who've Killed." *Minneapolis Star Tribune*, 2011.

Bell, David. *Staffordshire Tales of Murder & Mystery (Murder & Mystery)*, 2005.

Bemis, George. *Report of the Case of John W. Webster*, 1850.

"[The] Bicycle Bandit and the Brother Who Loved Him," Parts 1 to 3, *Old Colony History Museum*, 2018.

"Bicycle Highwayman." *New York Journal and Advertiser*, 1897.

"THE BICYCLE MURDERER; Willis Pleads Guilty to Murder in the Second Degree in Taunton, Mass." *The New York Times*, 1897.

Bleackley, Horace. *Trial of Jack Sheppard*, 1933.

Borchard, Edwin. "Frenchy"—Ameer Ben Ali." *State of New York, Public Papers of Governor Odell*, 1902.

Brendan, Rev. *Life, Crimes, and Confession of Bridget Durgan, the Fiendish Murderess of Mrs. Coriel: Whom She Butchered, Hoping to Take Her Place in the Affections of the Husband of Her Innocent and Lovely Victim*, 1867.

"Bridget Durgan." *Daily Evening Telegraph*, August 28, 1867.

"Bridget Durgan." *New York Herald*, August 28, 1867.

Briggs, Lloyd Vernon. *The Manner of Man That Kills: Spencer, Czolgosz, Richeson*, 1921.

Bryk, William. "Marm—a Gilded Age Mastermind." *New York Sun*, 2004.

Buckley, Matthew. "Sensations of Celebrity: Jack Sheppard and the Mass Audience," *Victorian Studies* 44(3) (Spring 2002).

"Burglar Lyons's Family; The Depravity of Its Youngest Member. He Abuses His Mother in a Police Court—Rewarding Her with Curses and Filthy Charges—Sorrows of a Woman Who Was Reared in Crime." *The New York Times*, 1880.

Byrnes, Thomas. *Professional Criminals of America*, 1886.

"Charley Ross Dead." *The Montreal Gazette*, 1943.

Cohen, Daniel A. *Pillars of Salt, Monuments of Grace: New England Crime Literature and the Origins of American Popular Culture, 1674–1860*, 2006.

Cohen, Patricia Cline. "The Helen Jewett Murder: Violence, Gender, and Sexual Licentiousness in Antebellum America," *NWSA Journal* (Summer 1990).

———. *The Murder of Helen Jewett*, 1998.

Conway, J. North. *Bag of Bones*, 2012.

———. "The Bicycle Bandit," *The Providence Journal* (2000).

———. *[The] Big Policeman*, 2010.

———. "The High Society Bank Robber of the 1800s." *The Daily Beast*, 2014.

———. *King of Heists*, 2009.

———. "Meet 'The Queen of Thieves' Marm Mandelbaum, New York City's First Mob Boss." *The Daily Beast*, 2014.

———. *Queen of Thieves*, 2014.

"The Coriel Murder." *World*, June 5, 1867.

"The Coriell Murder." *Trenton State Gazette*, May 22, 1867.

Cummings, Amos. "History of the Loomis Gang." *New York Sun*, 1877.

Daniels, Harriet McDougal. *Nine-Mile Swamp: A Story of the Loomis Gang*, 1941.

Dapson, Leon. "The Loomis Gang." *New York History*, 1938.

Defoe, Daniel. *The History of the Remarkable Life of John Sheppard: Containing a Particular Account of His Many Robberies and Escapes*, 1724.

DeWolf, Elizabeth. *The Murder of Mary Bean and Other Stories*, 2007.

"Dist Atty Pelletier Pleads for Pomeroy." *Boston Globe*, 1917.

Duke, Thomas. *The Murder of a Wealthy Boston Physician by a Harvard Professor, 1849*, 1910.

Fanebust, Wayne. *The Missing Corpse: Grave Robbing a Gilded Age Tycoon*, 2005.

Fox, Samuel, Patrick Lyon, and Thomas Lloyd. *Robbery of the Bank of Pennsylvania in 1798 the Trial in the Supreme Court of the State of Pennsylvania*, 1808.

Frasier, Isaac. *A Brief Account of the Life, and Abominable Thefts, of the Notorious Isaac Frasier*, 1768.

Gilbert, James. *The Trial of William Palmer for the Alleged Rugeley Poisonings*, 1856.

Gilfoyle, Timothy J. *City of Eros: New York City, Prostitution, and the Commercialization of Sex 1790–1920*, 1992.

Graves, Robert. *They Hanged My Saintly Billy: The Life and Death of Dr William Palmer*, 1957.

Hagen, Carrie. *We Is Got Him: The Kidnapping that Changed America*, 2011.

"Hartford, August 1." *Boston News-Letter*, August 4, 1768.

Hibbert, Christopher. *The Road to Tyburn: The story of Jack Sheppard and the Eighteenth-Century London Underworld*, 1957.

"Hint to a Murder Hid by Coroner's Aid." *The New York Times*, 1914.

Hobart, Noah. *Excessive Wickedness, the Way to an Untimely Death. A Sermon*, 1768

Holub, Rona. "Fredericka Mandelbaum." In *Immigrant Entrepreneurship: German-American Business Biographies, 1720 to the Present*, 2013.

Houdini, Harry. *The Right Way to Do Wrong: An Exposé of Successful Criminals*, 1906.

Howson, Gerald. *Thief-Taker General: Jonathan Wild and the Emergence of Crime and Corruption as a Way of Life in Eighteenth-Century England*, 1970.

"Jane Toppan's Crimes: Confessed to Killing Thirty-One Human Beings. Also Told Her Counsel She Set Fires and Committed Other Serious Offenses. Said She Was Not Insane Knew What She Was Doing and Therefore Could Not Be Mad." *Hoosier State Chronicles*, 2017.

"Jane Toppan's Moral Insanity." *Los Angeles Herald, 1904*.

Kasserman, David Richard. *Fall River Outrage: Life, Murder, and Justice in Early Industrial New England*, 1986.

Lardner, James and Thomas A. Reppetto. *NYPD: A City and Its Police*, 2017.

[The] Life of Helen Jewett. Illustrative of Her Adventures with Very Important Incidents, from her Seduction to the Period of Her Murder, Together with Various Extracts from Her Journal, Correspondence, and Poetical Effusions, 1836.

Lyon, Patrick. *The Narrative of Patrick Lyon: Who Suffered Three Months Severe Imprisonment in Philadelphia Gaol, on Merely a Vague Suspicion of Being Concerned in the Robbery of the Bank of Pennsylvania, with His Remarks Thereon*, 1799.

Lyons, Louis. "Records Show Jesse Pomeroy Never Did Deserve Sympathy." *Boston Globe*, 1932.

Lyons, Sophie. *Why Crimes Does Not Pay*, 1913.

Macintyre, Ben. *The Napoleon of Crime: The Life and Times of Adam Worth, Master Thief*, 1997.

Manaugh, Geoff. *A Burglar's Guide to the City*, 2016.

Marr, John. "The Terribly True Tale of the Youngest Girl Ever Executed in America." *Murder Can Be Fun*, 2015.

"[The] Middlesex Murder Case." *Trenton State Gazette*, May 1, 1867.

Miller, Reverend. *A Full and Complete Confession of the Horrid Transactions in the Life of George Hamilton: The Murderer of Mary Bean, the Factory Girl*, 1852.

"Miscellaneous." *New York Herald*, February 27, 1867.

Miss, J. A. B. *Mary Bean: The Factory Girl*, 1850.

Moore, Lucy. *The Thieves' Opera*, 1997.

"Murder in Newmarket, N. J." *New York Tribune*, February 27, 1867.

Myers, Jennifer. "For 10 Years, 'Jolly Jane' Poured Her Poison." *Lowell Sun*, 2011.

Nash, Jay Robert. *World Encyclopedia of 20th Century Murder*, 1992.

"New Haven." *Connecticut Journal*, April 8, 1768.

"New Haven." *Connecticut Journal*, April 29, 1768.

"New Haven." *Connecticut Journal*, July 29, 1768.

"New Haven." *Connecticut Journal*, August 29, 1768.

"New Haven." *Connecticut Journal*, September 9, 1768.

"[The] Newmarket Murder." *Trenton State Gazette*, May 23, 1867.

"[The] Newmarket Murder." *World*, May 31, 1867.

Paiva, Walter. "The Murder of Dr. George Parkman." *The Harvard Crimson*, 2017.

Papke, David Ray. *Framing the Criminal. Crime, Cultural Work, and the Loss of Critical Perspective, 1830–1900*, 1987.

"PEOPLE Explains: Infamous Kidnappings Throughout History." *People*, 2018.

"Philadelphia Boy Still Missing; Charlie Ross' Brother Declares Claim of Blair Ridiculous." *The Evening Independent*, 1939.

Phillips, Charles and Alan Axelrod. *Cops, Crooks, and Criminologists: An International Biographical Dictionary of Law Enforcement*, 2000.

Pinkerton, Allan. *Professional Thieves and the Detective: With a Sketch by the Author How He Became a Detective*, 1881.

"Poison Her Passion." *The Clinton Morning Age*, 1902.

"Pomeroy Going to State Farm." *Boston Globe*, 1929.

Pomeroy, Jesse Harding. *The Autobiography of Jesse Harding Pomeroy, Written by Himself*, 1875.

Porterfield, Waldon R. "Little Charlie and the Crime That Shocked the Nation." *Milwaukee Journal*, 1974.

Potier, Beth. "Murder at Harvard." *Harvard Gazette*, 2002.

Potts, Michael. *"Jane Toppan: A Greed, Power, and Lust Serial Killer."* *Academia*, 2017.

"Queen of Crooks Reforms; Mrs. Lyons-Burke Will Devote Half-Million to Aiding Convicts." *The New York Times*, April 13, 1913.

Raven, Rory. *Wicked Conduct: The Minister, the Mill Girl, and the Murder That Captivated Old Rhode Island*, 2009.

"Richeson Executed for Girl's Murder." *The New York Times*, 1912.

"Rob Ex-Confidence Woman; Burglars Sack Sophie L. Burke's Detroit Home—Get $20,000." *The New York Times*, 1922.

Ross, Christian. *The Father's Story of Charley Ross, the Kidnapped Child*, 1876.

Russell, Charles Edward. "Old Shakespeare." *Illustrated Detective Magazine*, 1931.

"[The] Scaffold." *Daily Evening Telegraph*, August 30, 1867.

Schechter, Harold. *Fiend: The Shocking Story of America's Youngest Serial Killer*, 2000.

Sifakis, Carl. *The Encyclopedia of American Crime, 2001*.

Skirboll, Aaron. *Thief-Taker Hangings: How Daniel Defoe, Jonathan Wild, and Jack Sheppard Captivated London and Created the Celebrity Criminal*, 2014.

"Sophie Lyons Offers Gift; Retired Thief Has Site for Criminals Home in Detroit." *The New York Times*, 1916.

Stagis, Julie. "A Girl, 12, Is Hanged in Connecticut for Murder in 1786." *Hartford Courant*, 2014.

Stone, James. *The Trial of Prof. John White Webster*, 1850.

Towne, Vincent. "Kidnapers Used Candy to Lure Charley Ross." *Pittsburgh Post-Gazette*, 1941.

Voss, Frederick and James Barber. *We Never Sleep: The First Fifty Years of the Pinkertons*, 1981.

Vanderlinden, Wolf, "The New York Affair." *Ripper Notes*: part one, 2003; parts two and three, 2004.

Walling, George Washington. *Recollections of a New York Chief of Police*, 1887.

Index

Stocker, John C., 33, 35, 38
Stokley, William, 126
"The Stolen White Elephant," 139
Stoude, Herman, 155
Strange, Fred, 187–89, 191
Suffolk County Superior Court, 193
suicide, 43–45, 197
Sullivan, Mary, 167
The Sun, 169
The Sun Building, 140
Sykes, James, 10

Taunton, Massachusetts, 187–90
Taunton Cycling Club, 187, 188
Taunton Daily Gazette, 188, 190
Taunton Insane Hospital, 169, 170
Taunton Lunatic Asylum, 170
Tew, James, 63–65
Tharme, Eliza, 95
Theological School, 165
"The Thief Taker General." *See* Wild, Jonathan
Third Baptist church, 198
Thompson, Connecticut, 48
Thornton, Ann, 94–96
The Three-penny Opera (Brecht and Weill), 12
Throgsneck, Long Island, 127
The Times, 178
Tiverton, Rhode Island, 43, 47, 50–54
Toppan, Ann, 165
Toppan, Elizabeth, 166, 167
Toppan, Jane, 165–71

Townsend, Rosina, 59–61, 63, 64, 66, 67
Tramp's Rock, Mott's Woods, 150
Tribune, 178
Twain, Mark, 139
Tweed, William Marcy "Boss," 158

Union Conscription Act (1863), 149
Union Fields Cemetery, 160
Union military service, 149
Union Poor Law workhouses, 116
United States. *See* America
University of Cincinnati, 148
University of Vienna, 180
US Constitution, 38
US Supreme Court, 29, 88
The Utica Daily Observer, 110
The Utica Oneida Weekly, 109

Van Brunt, Albert, 128, 129
Van Brunt, Holmes, 128, 129
Vanderbilt, Cornelius, 136, 145
Vreeland, Henry, 138

Walling, George Washington, 126, 129, 130, 160
Walnut Street Prison, 36, 39
Wanamaker, John, 140
Washington, George, 33
The Waterville Times, 109
Webster, John, 72–81
Weill, Kurt, 12
Westchester County, 139
Westervelt, William, 127, 130

About the Author

J. North Conway is the author of seventeen nonfiction books and is the recipient of the 2019 John Curtis Award for Lifelong Learning in honor of his entire body of work. Other awardees include David McCullough. His book *King of Heists* was chosen as one of the top five books of the summer of 2009 by *Readers' Digest*. He worked as a newspaper reporter and editor for twenty-five years and currently teaches at a small college in southeastern Massachusetts.

Other Books by the Author

Nonfiction

    Soldier Parrott, 2021
    The Wreck of the Portland, 2019
    New England Rocks: Historic Geological Wonders, 2017
    Outside Providence: Selected Poems, 2016
    Attack of the HMS Nimrod: Wareham and the War of 1812, 2014
    Queen of Thieves, 2014
    Bag of Bones, 2012
    The Big Policeman, 2010
    King of Heists, 2009
    The Cape Cod Canal: Breaking through the Bared and Bended Arm, 2008
    Head above Water, 2005
    Shipwrecks of New England, 2000
    New England Visionaries, 1998
    New England Women of Substance, 1996
    American Literacy: Fifty Books That Define Our Culture and Ourselves, 1994
    From Coup to Nuts: A Revolutionary Cookbook, 1987